Lines of Inquiry

Also by H. L. Hix

Poetry

First Fire, Then Birds *
Incident Light *
Legible Heavens *
God Bless *
Chromatic *
Shadows of Houses *
Surely As Birds Fly
Rational Numbers
Perfect Hell

Translations

Eugenijus Ališanka, *from unwritten histories*, trans. with the author
Jüri Talvet, *Of Snow, of Soul: New Selected Poems*, trans. with the author
Jüri Talvet, *Estonian Elegy: Selected Poems*, trans. with the author
Juhan Liiv, *The Mind Would Bear No Better*, trans. with Jüri Talvet
On the Way Home: An Anthology of Contemporary Estonian Poetry, trans. with Jüri Talvet
Jüri Talvet, *A Call for Cultural Symbiosis*, trans. with the author
Eugenijus Ališanka, *City of Ash*, trans. with the author

Anthologies

New Voices: Contemporary Poetry from the United States
Wild and Whirling Words: A Poetic Conversation *

Theory and Criticism

As Easy As Lying: Essays on Poetry *
Understanding William H. Gass
Understanding W. S. Merwin
Spirits Hovering Over the Ashes: Legacies of Postmodern Theory
Morte d'Author: An Autopsy

* Also published by Etruscan Press

Lines of Inquiry

H. L. HIX

etruscan press

Etruscan Press
Wilkes University
84 West South Street
Wilkes-Barre, PA 18766
(570) 408-4546

WILKES UNIVERSITY

www.etruscanpress.org

Published 2011 by Etruscan Press
Printed in the United States of America
Cover design by Julianne Popovec
Interior design and typesetting by Kanae Otsubo & Julianne Popovec
The text of this book is set in Adobe Caslon Pro.

Library of Congress Cataloging-in-Publication Data

Hix, H. L.
  Lines of inquiry / H.L. Hix. -- 1st ed.
    p. cm.
  ISBN 978-0-9832944-0-5 (alk. paper)
  I. Title.
  PS3558.I88L55 2011
  811'.54--dc23
                            2011034201

First Edition
11 12 13 14 15 5 4 3 2 1

This book is printed on recycled, acid-free paper.

Lines of Inquiry

Attributions

The epigraph to "Take You a Course, Get You a Place" is from Jeanette Winterson, *Art [Objects]*.

The epigraphs to the sections are from the following sources:
"Is": Flannery O'Connor, *Mystery and Manners*.
"Is Not": Tadao Ando, in Michael Auping, *Seven Interviews with Tadao Ando*.
"Is Too": Nicholas Mosley, *Inventing God*.

Acknowledgments

The inquiries collated here invite conversation, but also result from it. Which makes me grateful to a number of conversation partners.

For "Sparrows and Fireworks and Ruins" I am grateful to Terri Witek, editor of the "Poet of the Month" website (poetrynet.org) for offering it occasion, and to Kate Northrop, Judi Ross, and Benito Hernández, my conversation partners on Monte Alban. • "Something More" evokes my gratitude to my colleagues in the MFA program and the English Department at the University of Wyoming, with whom I am privileged to be in ongoing conversation, and to Robert Nazarene (another fan of Johnny Cash's late work) for publishing it in *Margie*. • "Four Charges," too, arose in conversation with my colleagues, at the annual forum with which we, the students and teachers in the MFA program, mark the beginning of each academic year by charging one another with our collective expectations. I have not tried to remove the indicators of connection to that occasion and that community. • "Take You a Course, Get You a Place" exists thanks to those responsible for creating and sustaining a conversation, in the form of a faculty exchange, between the University of Wyoming and Shanghai University, especially Dean Oliver Walter, Dean Tao Feiya, and Dr. Yarong Ashley. Its final form is due in part to conversation with William Thompson, who published a version of it in the *Alabama Literary Review*.

For occasioning "Ninety-five Theses," I am grateful to George Szirtes, whom I have not met, but with whose essay in *Poetry* a few years back I disagreed heartily enough to try to say why. For giving it a place in a conversation on the aphorism in *Hotel Amerika*, I am grateful to David Lazar. • "If Design Govern" began as notes for workshops, one on experimental form and another on the sonnet, at the West Chester poetry conference: it owes thanks to Michael Peich for lending me the workshops, and to the workshops' participants for bartering back better ideas than I brought them, a courtesy compounded for an early version of the essay by visitation from the eyes of a better scholar than I have been, David Caplan, and a better poet, Kate Northrop. • "Occasions" joins the conversation that is the book *Poet's Bookshelf II*, edited by Peter Davis and Tom Koontz. • "Winter Syntax" owes thanks to Christian Wiman for including it in the conversation he has made of *Poetry* magazine.

Friendships and conversations with visual artists have been among the most inspiring and sustaining I have known, and I thank the artists whose work is discussed here, in addition to the editors, museum directors, gallery owners, and curators responsible for commissioning and/or publishing the essays in "Dimensions," earlier versions of which were reviews of exhibitions, or contributions to exhibition catalogs. Images of work discussed in "Dimensions" may be viewed at the *Lines of Inquiry* entry at www.hlhix.com. • The interviews by John Poch and Philip Metres continue conversations that had already begun, and friendships for which I am grateful. I thank the *AWP Chronicle* for publishing one of those interviews, and *Jacket* magazine (jacketmagazine.com) for publishing the other. • Two streams converge in the letters that end this book. For nearly twenty years, ever since her *Lyric Philosophy* prompted me to write her a fan letter, I have savored a conversation by correspondence with Jan Zwicky, though seldom in that time have we been able to converse face-to-face. For two of those years, I wrote all my correspondence—to Jan and to others—in "verse" epistles. Both streams, the correspondence with Jan and the verse epistles, were intended to be private, but the stretch in which the two streams converge seemed so clearly "lines of inquiry" that I asked Jan for permission to make them open letters. At one point, the "March 2003" letter, the two streams converge with a third, a correspondence (then in typescript but now published as *Contemplation & Resistance*) between Jan and another poet, Tim Lilburn, so the ideas and passages I cite in my letter include hers and his, not sorted by source. My letters to Jan *attempt* (successfully or not) to contribute to our conversation something—in words I borrow not from one of her letters but from one of her poems—"precise and nameless as that river / scattering itself among / the frost and rocks."

For a conversation that extends, beyond particular essays, across books, I am indebted to my editor and friend Phil Brady, who—as poet and essayist alike—is *il miglior fabbro*. • For the conversation that is the making of a life together, one owes that particular gratitude we name love: I am indebted so to Kate.

Lines of Inquiry

Rationale

As a reader of poetry, and a viewer of art, I do not cultivate "disinterestedness," that dubious Eliotic critical ideal, but instead live under the spell of such mantras as these: Harold Bloom: "The meaning of a poem can only be another poem." Rilke: "Works of art are of an infinite loneliness and with nothing so little to be reached as with criticism. Only love can grasp and hold and be just toward them." Schlegel: "A critical judgment of an artistic production has no civil rights in the realm of art if it isn't itself a work of art." Jan Zwicky: Truth "is the result of *attention*. (As opposed to inspection.) Of looking informed by love."

Explanation and evaluation more often follow inspection than attention, and do not exhaust the valid aims of criticism. (Or if they do, then criticism is not the only valid mode of discursive response to poetry.) One might as worthily pursue instead such non-explanatory and only indirectly evaluatory aims as: to extend the associations made in the poem, to fulfill the poem's "logic of metaphor," to follow out its suggestions, to contextualize the poem, to express in response to the poem wonderment and joy or irritation and disdain.

If a poem or a painting resembles a joke in that you get it or you don't, then explanation ought to be the last resort of criticism, because it can occur only when the poem/joke is deprived of its best effect, and only as a cause of that deprivation. Explanation identifies the conditions which, had they held in one prior to the joke, would have allowed one to enjoy it. Explanation *replaces* laughter. I prefer instead a criticism that seeks to be the barroom and the second gin and tonic that help create the mood of attunement in which the stand-up comic's funny lines provoke a good laugh.

When Heidegger sets out to "bring into relief phenomenally the unitary primordial structure of the being of Da-sein," he acknowledges but cannot simply apply Aristotelian analysis or Kantian critique. He perceives his work not primarily as explanation but as taking care, something like an ecology of being, and talks not about mastery and comprehension but about attunement, "a disclosive submission to world out of which things that matter to us can be encountered." Similarly, my ambition in this book is not analysis or critique of the work, but attunement to it, a "disclosive submissiveness" through which things that matter to us—law and grace; war and peace; pity and fear; faith, hope, and love; remembrance of things past—can be sought, not by inspection but by attention.

Such an ecology of the poem, a taking care of it, taking note of it, this book attempts to act out as a principle. The question of success at its ambition makes no more sense than it does in relation to physical ecology. That I cannot "succeed" at taking care of the biosphere by recycling newspapers and carpooling (or even that—from laziness, say—I *do* not succeed) does not diminish the obligation to orient myself toward that goal. In this book I have oriented myself by joining certain long traditions: that of the verse essay, Horace to Pope to Perelman, with the particular kind of "taking care" that it entails; the dialogical tradition of philosophy, on whose metaphorical stage Plato impersonated a Socrates who might have thought as such a person must, as today on the (more modest) stage of the interview one might impersonate as well as one can a poet who is as one wishes one were; the tradition of inquiry into art, on the premise that visual artists' lives are sisters to my own; and the epistolary tradition.

Exposition, the laying out (ex-) of one position, surely has its worth, but I have chosen instead to treat poems and works of visual art as provisions for a journey, and thus to treat these essays each as provisional. I am not now in the same place (literally or figuratively) as when I wrote the first of these pieces. I understand poetry, its purposes and possibilities, differently now. So I stand by nothing of what follows; *standing by* ideas seems to me the wrong response to them. Treating them as markers on a path, each to be left behind in pursuit of another, seems more of a piece with a pilgrim's progress. So, for instance, the list of sonnets celebrated and cerebrated in "If Design Govern" differs from the list I would construct today, and I will have failed of my commitments if the list I would construct next year did not differ yet more. I *want* such provisionality. I would write different essays now, but the ones I wrote provided for me. May they provide for you.

Is

No matter what particular country it is, it is inside as well as outside.

Sparrows and Fireworks and Ruins

As I write this, sparrows scuffle on the skylight.
    Or maybe they're merely taking dust baths:
the skylight's translucency prevents my *seeing*
    the birds, and surely in so dry a place
dust collects at the skylight's rim. In any case,
    the convex skylight amplifies the sound
so that it fills the whole apartment my partner
    and I are renting, in which sounds echo
over the cement and tile floors and plaster walls.
    In rain the skylight leaks a little, leaves
puddles in the stairwell that make the hard stairs slick.

    It is a Sunday morning, still early.
At six, in the plaza of Santa Domingo,
    the cathedral barely a block away,
fireworks began. Not the light show Americans
    associate with Independence Day,
not something to be seen at all but to be heard,
    each a high whistle sliding swiftly down
an octave or so, then BOOM. In a few minutes
    bells followed the fireworks, not with stately
tolling of the hour but as if sounding alarm,
    or as if the swinging of those bells' ropes
were a contest with the bellman who labors at
    La Sangre de Cristo, just down the street,
a small, vigorous silhouette visible through
    the openings atop the bell towers.

Yesterday my partner and I, with an old friend,
    an artist I hadn't seen in ten years,
visited Monte Alban, a high mountain ridge
    with sublime vistas all around, and crowned
with monumental architecture, a complex
    of ancient ruins partially restored.

Now an archeological site, this mountain
        was for two thousand years—from 500
BCE to around 1500 CE—
        capital of the Zapotec Empire.

It's July. I'm here in Oaxaca for two weeks,
        for Spanish lessons. My having taken
beginning classes at my university
        means that, in principle if not in fact,
I can conjugate, in each tense, regular verbs
        and the most common irregular ones,
but I'm middle-aged and those classes far too large,
        so I haven't made much progress. I hope
even this short immersion will help. Not counting
        a month cloistered among English speakers
at a residency in Spain years back, this is
        my first stay in a Spanish-speaking land.

A week ago, waiting at the Denver airport
        to check in, the woman in front of me
turned for some idle chat. "Where ya headed," she asked.
        She and her three traveling companions—
her husband, I supposed, and another couple—
        were buoyant, laughing and talking loudly.
They looked like recent retirees, each with a big
        set of golf clubs to be checked. "Mexico,"
I said. She smiled at our kinship. We'd share a flight,
        as I knew from their loud conversation.
But then—I had no golf clubs, no tennis rackets—
        she looked for some assurance. "Cabo, right?"

One might travel for various reasons, and I
        would be wrong to dismiss hers or to find
in my own too smug a satisfaction. Problems
        with my travel are obvious enough,
starting with the jet fuel burned just as much for me

on our flight as for her. Still, her reasons
and mine do differ. She travels to make her life
    at least briefly more as it ought to be,
to restore Eden, approximate Paradise.
    I travel to make my life briefly more
as it actually is. Each of us desires
    to heighten a set of conditions: she,
those that secure her as owner and consumer
    of her life, her world; I, those that clarify
my condition as resident alien.
    For her, travel offers buffets, beaches,
and green fees included in the package at one
    low price, needs met and all desires fulfilled
without obligations to interfere, others
    like oneself with whom to share the pleasures,
visibly different others to cook and clean
    and drive and leave a pretty chocolate
on the pillow at night when they turn down the bed.
    For me, travel gives instead conditions
to recognize as my own and people to see
    as myself. Sparrows, fireworks, and ruins,
visible ribcages of dogs roaming the streets.

    So with poetry. One might seek in it
confirmation that god's in his heaven and all's
    right with the world. I seek in poetry
to find what I didn't know I was looking for.
    One might seek in poetry assurance
from the familiar that all is as we've always
    known it to be. I seek in poetry
to be *de*familiarized, estranged, to have
    what I take for granted taken away.
That ever unfamiliar world offers me less
    security, but enforces more awe.

Something More:
Notes Toward a Writing Pedagogy

On the last CD he made before his death, Johnny Cash
has enough trouble breathing that he has hardly any
dynamic range; he practically talks rather than sings;
and he can't sustain a note for any real duration.
Any glee club member could record the songs with greater
technical fluency. But something more going on there,
something beyond technique, lends weight to Cash's performance.
His inability to sustain a note, for instance,
lends poignancy to his cover of Roberta Flack's song,
"The First Time Ever I Saw Your Face." What in her version
are long sustained notes, in his version become long pauses
between notes. The gravitas of a recognizably
elderly voice recalling "the first time ever I saw
your face" overwhelms the inability quite to reach
the right note at the end of the phrase "I thought the sun rose
in your eyes." One thinks of Gaunt's lines from *Richard II*:
>   … the tongues of dying men
>   Enforce attention like deep harmony.
>   Where words are scarce, they are seldom spent in vain,
>   For they breathe truth that breathe their words in pain.
       Cash's mortality, joined to his and our awareness
of it, outweighs the technical flaws in his performance,
which suggests, as a basic psychological problem
for any writing program, that the most crucial feature
of a writer is not technique or craft, but "something more,"
some ineffable quality not common but unique
to each writer, concocted of various elements
such as desire and curiosity and obsession,
that makes her persist in the work with or without reward,
that purifies the ambitions and hones the attentions,
that sends the mind, a hungry coyote, into the world.
       One might nod to that intimidating state of affairs
by keeping one's pedagogical ambitions modest,

teaching only technique and craft, and leaving one's students
on their own for the rest. Maybe that's enough. After all,
there are students who possess the "something more" already,
or will acquire it on their own. I certainly agree
that teaching technique is a *necessary* condition
for sound writing pedagogy. But if, as I believe,
it is not *sufficient,* then we must also "tell it slant":
point toward that ineffable but crucial something more
by teaching something more. If a program or professor
wants, and is willing to *risk,* something more for the students
than to normalize and credential them, wants to arm them
beyond a skill set and a socially acceptable
contributor's note, the next question is *how* to do so.
    The standard creative writing curriculum is built
on "workshop." Iowa and other distinguished programs
demonstrate the virtues of this approach, which I value,
but the hegemony of which I wish to undermine,
by noting not workshop's flaws but its partiality,
its pedagogical limitations. Workshop, when and if
it works, works through context, achieving its most profound
effect on the student when, and because, it is only
one among several modes of instruction. The workshop
is a method, but *its* method is to correct or shape.
This has tremendous value, we all need it, and we all
find it one way or another even outside of school:
one's agent or editor; one's colleagues; rejection slips.
By itself, though, correction could bring about nothing but
uniformity and conformity. We all must learn
the rules of the language games called fiction and poetry,
and correction helps in that process, but writers also
challenge those rules, and correction can't help such resistance.
    We learn by being corrected, surely, but we learn, too,
by being informed, provoked, nurtured. We learn from research,
from reading, from questioning and being questioned. We learn
by imitating models. We learn by observation
and immersion. We learn—though I recommend against its

planned inclusion in a curriculum—through suffering:
"Anguish," Bataille insists, "is no less than intelligence
the means for knowing." So we who claim to teach writing owe
our students a multi-dimensional experience
the coursework and methodologies of which include
but are not limited to, may not even emphasize, workshops.
We owe our students numerous and various models:
lit courses; theory courses; coursework that frames writing
in broad cultural contexts; coursework on subjects beyond
literature, that gives other conceptual substance
to inform their work; coursework on the elements and tools
of writing, such as grammar, logic, etymology;
and models other than coursework, such as community
hosted within and beyond the program. Thus enriching
each participant's background, we enrich workshop itself.
    Louis Mackey defines poetry as "the aesthetic
manifestation of the ironic diremption of
essence and phenomenon." Poetry, in other words,
is the way the gap between how things are and how they seem
shows itself. (Mackey's definition occurs in a book
about Kierkegaard, and refers not to poetry as
distinct from fiction, but to poetry as distinct from
analytical philosophy, say, or history.
He is speaking, in other words, of a category
that *includes* fiction, the category we often call
"creative writing.") Mackey's definition implies that
a writer needs, and we should seek to seed in our students,
the sort of sensibility not settled simply in
either essence or phenomenon, but alert to both,
traveling restlessly back and forth between them, able
to make its own maps of the crossing, to make its own songs
and stories in which, as in Blake, "contraries meet in one."
Such duplicity—multiplicity—of perspective,
if not itself the something more, may open onto it.
    The diremption Mackey postulates can also be framed
in existential terms. Rousseau blamed unhappiness on

"disproportion between our desires and our faculties."
In a society aimed first at enlarging that gap
by multiplying our desires, then offering relief
for the artificially magnified gap through the sale
of sedatives (television, Prozac, "consumer goods"),
resistance might mean, instead of multiplying desires,
to elevate the faculties. Louise Glück argues that
"deft skirting" of despair (her term for the disproportion
between our desires and our faculties) creates "a life
lived on the surface, intimidated by depth, a life
that refuses to be used by time, which it tries instead
to dominate or evade." Pedagogy in writing
(and pedagogy across the humanities and arts)
aims to grant students alternatives to society's
attempt to multiply desires, diminish faculties,
and sell sedatives. It attempts to equip students—us—
to confront despair instead of trying to evade it.

Which returns to my hypothesis that what *conditions*
writing may matter more than even the writing itself
and such elements as technique and craft. Iris Murdoch,
as part of a discussion of ethics, argues against
the existentialist illusion of an absolute
freedom to act, noting that not the choice itself but what
conditions the choice determines its ethical value.
She whose mind it never crosses to shoplift, Murdoch claims,
is better than he who, tempted, merely chooses not to.
Instead of being "switched off in between the occurrence
of explicit moral choices," the moral life "goes on
continually." What matters most is not the choices,
but what happens between them. Extending Murdoch's claim
to writing would mean creation of stories or poems
is not confined to the moment of writing, but goes on
continually. The scope of our charge, the *presumption*
of it, should give us pause: we ought not teach students only
how to make valid claims in the moment of writing,
but how to create for themselves a background against which,
more than choice, an inevitability is at work.

Of the ways one might name that inevitability
that precludes choice, Agnes Martin selects "inspiration":
"While you have a choice," she says, "that is not inspiration.
If a decision is required, that is not inspiration
and you should not do anything by decision." Jack Gilbert's
"In Dispraise of Poetry" ends with a related claim,
namely that "the gift could not be refused." It may be that
the students able to receive the gift will receive it
whether or not it is we who tender it. Which demands
of us a certain modesty before *all* our students:
acknowledgment of disproportion between our desire
to grant them the gift, and our faculties, which do not rise
to that level. Between two poles—that we are our students'
last best hope, their Virgilian guides to harrow the hell
of a stultifying, humanity-sapping culture,
and that we are but minor tools of that necessity
that urges our students into lives of reinventing
their worlds and ours—we are surely closer to the latter.
     That our role be modest does not preclude our yet being
party to that miracle (what else to call it?) by which
the false—in prose fiction, or in poetry's "supreme fiction"—
reveals true and vital things about oneself or the world.
How can the false show us the true? Answering that question
would give another ground for pedagogy, something like
Mackey's vision of writing as ironic diremption.
There are many possibilities. Eudora Welty
talks of a kind of binocular vision that in its
multiplication of points of view resembles Mackey's
definition: "The fictional eye," she says, "sees in, through,
and around what is really there." In other words, the real
and the true are not coterminous. So the "something more"
we seek is an altered relation to the world. Again,
now in Jeanette Winterson's words, "The fiction, the poem,
is not a version of the facts, it is an entirely
different way of seeing." And that would give to writing
the purpose Donald Barthelme formulates in this way:

"It's our good fortune to be able to imagine
alternative realities, other possibilities.
We can quarrel with the world, constructively." Barthelme,
Winterson, and Welty agree on the capacity
fiction has for re-vision of the world. Remembering
Socrates' words from Plato's *Phaedrus*, that "it is noble
to pursue a noble purpose, whatever the outcome,"
may tender consolation: even to *seek* to offer
students that capacity for re-vision of the world,
though we be uncertain *how* to do so, may be worthy.

Four Charges

1.

You're not here to study writing, and I'm not here to teach it.

I don't say that facetiously, though of course I don't mean it quite at face value, either. In saying it I want to register three specific meanings. I'll deal at greater length with the first than with the second and the third, so don't become alarmed, fearing that I'll drone on endlessly.

In the *Physics,* Aristotle distinguishes between material, formal, efficient, and final causes. Your studying writing and my teaching writing are what Aristotle calls the *efficient* cause of our being here: the immediate agency producing the result. Studying writing (rather than, say, working on an oil rig) has you here (rather than on the Gulf Coast or in Alaska). But studying or teaching writing ought not, I submit, be the *final* cause of our being here. Aristotle describes the final cause as the end, "'that for the sake of which' a thing is done, e.g. health is the [final] cause of [exercise]." You don't exercise for the sake of exercising; you exercise because doing so contributes to health. So should it be with writing.

To say this more simply, I think your studying and my teaching ought to be means to other ends, but not ends in themselves. I think, further, that it behooves us to choose those ends reflectively, because some ends are worthier than others. A couple of obvious examples will stand for a whole range of unworthy ends. Fame, for instance, would be an ill-chosen end, not only because it is a vanity (Ben Jonson calls it a "toy," Milton calls it the "last infirmity of noble minds"), but also because it's so improbable. More golfers are struck by lightning each year than writers achieve anything that could justly be called fame. If fame is what you seek, drop the study of writing now and go audition for *Star Search*—your odds would be better. Money, similarly, would be an ignoble end to pursue, and for similar reasons: money itself has value only as a means and not as an end, and if it's unlikely that writing will make you famous, it's even more unlikely that it will make you rich.

You can tell where I'm going with this: not toward discouraging you from an enterprise to which obviously I myself am deeply committed, but recommending a kind of non-religious correlative to the injunction from the biblical "Sermon on the Mount" not to "lay up for yourselves treasures on earth, where moth and rust consume and where thieves break in and steal," but instead to "lay up for yourselves treasures in heaven." I recommend, in other words, deliberate choice of worthy ends toward which to direct your study of writing. Fortunately, there are healthy alternatives to fame and money and other trivial, self-serving, base, deceptive ends. Let me mention a few, as they have been articulated and claimed by notable recent writers.

One might pursue, for instance, personal transformation. The kind of self-knowledge Auden says writing potentially advances, when he admonishes us to "first discover what manner of person you are, and then learn to see everything through the lens of your gift," the transformation effected when such self-knowledge combines with the *dynamis*—the explosive force—George Oppen attributes to art when he calls it "the most violent of all actions," and says "it means to break thru that which has contained us. That which without art would contain us as it contains a plant."

That kind of personal transformation counts as a worthy end itself, but also has a public correlative that is equally worthy, and not independent of it. Writing can participate in political transformation because, in Donald Barthelme's formulation, writers are "able to imagine alternative realities, other possibilities. We can quarrel with the world, constructively." Imagining alternative realities does not occur without cost. Joseph Brodsky, whose life as a Soviet citizen made his awareness of those costs acute, tells why: "A poet gets into trouble because of his linguistic, and, by implication, his psychological superiority, rather than because of his politics. A song is a form of linguistic disobedience . . . [that] casts a doubt on a lot more than a concrete political system: it questions the entire existential order. And the number of its adversaries grows proportionally." That political transformation through writing may endanger the writer does not soften the imperative to pursue it, because if Vaclav Havel is right, the call to political transformation is simply the call to truth. "If the main pillar of the system is living a lie, then it is not surprising that the fundamental threat to it is living the truth. . . . Important events in the real world—whether admirable or monstrous—always have their prologue in the realm of words. . . . Responsibility for and towards words is . . . intrinsically ethical." Words, regardless of the size of their audience, are public, and there is no more important civic responsibility than to enact the integrity of the language.

Our integrity as individuals and the integrity of our society are inseparable, and our integrity as individuals cannot be separated from the acuity of our language. "It has become very plain," Laura (Riding) Jackson declares, "that we can have nothing genuinely new in our civilization—cannot have a new civilization—without a new scrupulousness in our linguistic functioning, that puts our every attitude of mind to the tests of human soundness that words alone can surely make." It is important in this context to recall another fact about writing's public role that implies another possible end to be pursued. Adrienne Rich insists that *your* seeing the truth and speaking it supports *my* seeing the truth and speaking it. "Women," she notes, "have often felt insane when cleaving to the truth of our experience. Our future depends on the sanity of each of us, and we have a profound stake, beyond the personal, in the project of describing our reality as candidly and fully as we can to each other." Your experience, and your truthful embrace of it, bears on your own life, yes, but bears also on the lives of others and their ability to embrace their own experience truthfully.

The ends you might pursue through the study of writing can be framed in philosophical terms. Metaphysically, as the reconciliation of human fugacity with cosmic duration, an end Blake implies writing can accomplish when he asserts that "Eternity is in love with the productions of time." Epistemologically, by reconciling the world one perceives with the world in itself, an end Leslie Scalapino thinks writing should pursue through "a dismantling of perception—so that hierarchical structure is not that perceiving—[that] changes occurrence itself." Ethically, in the terms Iris Murdoch articulates in her philosophical works, contending that art "teaches us how real things can be looked at and loved without being seized and used, without being appropriated into the greedy organism of the self." Because, as she puts it, "it is a *task* to come to see the world as it is," writing becomes moral. "*How* we see our situation," she says, "is itself, already, a moral activity."

The study of writing can bring about ends that benefit oneself. It can liberate one from the hypercommercialization that poisons contemporary culture: after noting the aimlessness of capital, the "sole purpose [of which] is to produce more in order to consume more," Octavio Paz calls poetry "the antidote to technology and the market." Writing can grant one traits of character one desires, as Camus suggests when he says that "Of all the schools of patience and lucidity, creation is the most effective." Writing can also give gifts to others, something Muriel Rukeyser claims as an end when she says that "the more clearly one writes, the more clearly will both the writer and the reader feel."

The range of worthy aims toward which your study of writing might be directed has no limits. It includes all the worthy ends one could pursue in *any* life, including ends not always associated with writing, such as love. Josephine Jacobsen says that observation, the central act that attends writing, when "raised to a certain degree," which writing facilitates, "is a kind of love." Jan Zwicky calls "ontological attention," her name for the state of mind a writer attempts to cultivate, "a form of love. When we love a thing," she says, "we can experience our responsibility toward it as limitless (the size of the world). Responsibility is the trace, in us, of the pressure of the world that is focused in a *this*. That is *how much* it is possible to attend; that is how large complete attention would be." If I were trying to formulate as succinctly as possible my own aim, I would borrow those words from Zwicky: *complete attention*. I am not here to teach writing, I am here to cultivate complete attention. Writing, and teaching writing, just happens to further the process.

The second meaning I want to register through saying, "You're not here to study writing, and I'm not here to teach it," is that I consider it counter to the studying and teaching of writing to "go through the motions." Complete attention would include questioning the presuppositions and processes one's culture (or subculture) inculcates. The immediate consequence for me, as it bears on my practice as a teacher and your experience as a student, is that I will not use a "workshop" approach to my writing "workshops." I will, or we can, talk more in those workshops themselves about why I will adopt an alternative pedagogy, but suffice it for now to say that I believe the collective scrutiny of purportedly important works, combined with other forms of collective inquiry, offers more benefit to you, immediately and long-term, than does group discussion of one another's work.

The final meaning I want to register through saying, "You're not here to study writing, and I'm not here to teach it," is that I think we want to acknowledge one of the limits we face in this enterprise. You and I both know what it means for me to say to you that I *can't* teach you to write. I can do many things that may contribute to your development as a writer: I can train my own background and judgment on your work, I can direct your attention to models you may find valuable, I can tender provocative points of view that may open new directions in your thinking, and so on. But none of those is teaching you to write, exactly. In algebra, I can show you, directly, how to solve for a variable, and your solving for that variable will mimic mine. Not so with writing, where a higher-order hermeneutic is happening in the gap between my teaching and your learning. Your level of responsibility, activity, and self-determination is higher.

I urge on you reflectiveness about the implications of that limit. For me, one thing to which it relates is my sense that writing has much more to do with preparation and decision than with inspiration (or that inspiration is composed largely of preparation and decision, whichever formulation you prefer). I despair of contributing in any direct or meaningful way to your "inspiration," an inner necessity that must already have claimed you or you wouldn't be here. Instead, I will focus my teaching on ways in which I believe I can further your preparation and aid in your decision making. For you, I hope it means you will be alert to the various ways in which you can further your development as a writer during your time in this program. We the faculty hope to be of value to you in your pursuit, but the paradox of the impossibility of teaching writing serves as a reminder that plenty of other aspects of the program may be just as important to you as we are: the visiting writers who pass through, the examples you find for yourself in your research, the things you learn in elective class-work in other disciplines, the stimulation of your peers, and so on.

I ask for your support of and challenge to my pursuit of complete attention, and I count it a privilege to be invited into your pursuit of the noble ends toward which I trust you have aimed your study of writing.

2.

For various reasons I am proud to be affiliated with this faculty. One reason is that they are outstanding writers. As this stack of books reveals, there are among them no slackers. They have published with such presses as Norton, Graywolf, and Basic Books, and they have been recognized by such awards as the Yale Series of Younger Poets Prize, the Rome Prize, the Southern Book Critics Circle Award, and fellowships from the National Endowment for the Arts.

But from the perspective of a student in the program, and from my perspective as director of the program, another fact about this faculty equals the importance of their impressive writing credentials, namely their commitment to teaching. I seldom pass Brad's office door, for instance, or Vicki's, when they are not engaged in critical dialogue with a student over his or her work. And I know from the reports of colleagues and friends who graduated from or are on the faculties of other MFA programs that such strong commitment to teaching, uniformly across a faculty, is by no means a normal attribute of MFA programs. MFA faculty members everywhere are committed, as they should be, to themselves and their own work. This faculty, though, to a degree far beyond the norm, is also committed to you and your work.

The characteristic on which I want to focus these remarks bears on that commitment to teaching. I am proud that, to a person, this faculty *reflects* on its teaching. Nothing demands that a creative writing teacher do so: pedagogy in writing programs is more or less given, and nearly universal. Our program reflects that givenness in its curriculum, in which the largest block of credit hours is devoted to workshops. The easiest approach would be simply to take teaching methodology for granted, but none of us do. Some members of this faculty have, as a result of thoughtful consideration, adopted workshop methodology "straight," some modify it, and some use alternative methodologies, but every faculty member here reflects, actively and on an ongoing basis, on her or his approach to teaching. The givenness of workshop methodology, though, also means that you as students likely expect it, so as one of the faculty members who does *not* use workshop methodology, I would like to speak to *why* I do not.

My adoption of alternative methodology does not result from skepticism about the results of workshopping. One need not look far to find validation for the workshop methodology. That so high a percentage of literary writers active today were educated in workshops suggests that workshop must produce results.

Workshops work for teaching writing. But so do horses and camels work for getting humans from place to place, and that did not oblige humans to use them exclusively; we now also use bicycles, cars, and airplanes. Comparison with pedagogy in other fields suggests alternatives to workshop. Consider music, for example. The curriculum of a graduate degree in music performance, whether voice or clarinet, classical or jazz, is built around three key ingredients: music history, music theory, and private instruction. There's a rationale to that trio. Music history is synthetic, far-sighted, in pursuit of breadth, looking beyond the current moment to precedents, beyond one's own culture to correlatives, and beyond the art per se to its contexts and purposes. Music theory is analytic, nearsighted, in pursuit of depth, looking more and more closely at elements and techniques, identifying, gathering, and integrating the building blocks of the medium, out of which works are composed and through which they are performed. Finally, private instruction is tutorial, overseeing the assimilation of the knowledge of history and theory into practice.

The analogy between music instruction and writing instruction allows me to formulate succinctly my rationale for not adopting the workshop method. I perceive MFA instruction as too light on the analytic aspect. Electives and literature classes, especially those designed with the history of literature as the basic framework, seem most closely analogous to music history, in that they examine context. Workshops, internships, and thesis, insofar as all take *your* work as the starting point, seem most closely analogous to private instruction. But that leaves nothing in the curriculum to undertake the role music theory plays in music instruction: the analytical role of discovering and evaluating the tools and elements of the medium. To pursue the mechanical metaphor for one more sentence: you might well get by with your tools in a bag on your back, reaching around when you need one, fumbling around blindly and pulling out a few until you find one that works, but you will be more efficient if you know what each tool is for and where it is stored, if you have an orderly tool chest with socket wrenches here and screwdrivers there, and a pegboard with little outlines for the drill and the saw, if in other words you have full knowledge of and immediate access to the tools of your trade.

(By the way, this alerts you to one of my prejudices in advising. Since the curriculum allows you to take anything with your elective hours, students tend to load up on workshops. I think that's a mistake, and I recommend against it. Because there is only so much you can practice in a semester as a musician, and only so much you can draft as a writer, the tutorial element is best spread out over time, not concentrated too heavily. It wouldn't be in your best interest at Julliard to take all private instruction, and it doesn't make sense here to take all workshops. You can only take so much out of the account without putting some back in. I recommend using the curriculum to make more deposits and fewer withdrawals during your time here.)

I look forward to enacting a tutorial role for some of you in relation to your theses. But I think a balance of synthetic, analytic, and tutorial is a sound approach to a writing pedagogy, so for the rest of my teaching in the program, beyond thesis advising, I feel obliged to address the void I perceive where I think an analytical component should be, and therefore will approach my "workshops" *not* as primarily tutorial, but as primarily analytical.

I hope that you are hearing in all the sets of remarks being offered here implicit challenges toward harder study and better writing, even where the challenges are not explicit. No doubt you have heard the implicit challenge in my remarks, which now in closing I make explicit: just as the faculty are reflective about how they are teaching, so I urge you to be reflective about how you are learning. Such reflectiveness will make your experience of this program richer, will draw more of the experience within the influence of your will. To appeal once more to the musical analogy, those of you who have studied a musical instrument will know that true expertise is developed not only by practicing *a lot*, but also by practicing *well*. Practicing a long time and with much effort but with bad habits only reinforces and ingrains one's errors and technical failings. A reflective approach to your study of writing will increase the odds that you are practicing well.

Graduate study is dialogical and research-based. The faculty will not be the only ones issuing implicit challenges this year. As you are my students, so am I your student. Thank you for the challenges you have offered me and will offer, and for the insights you have given me and will give.

3.

The phrase "coming out" refers to the dangerous but liberating assertion of sexual identity, as in a debutante's scripted "coming out" into society or a homosexual's "coming out" from a closeted life. Though education is less explicitly and exclusively about sexuality, it too is a coming out: the word *education*, as probably you know, comes from a Latin verb/prefix combination meaning "to lead out." And education is just as dangerous and just as liberating as any other coming out.

But education is not homogenous. To take as examples the extremes, a kindergarten education and a PhD differ radically in subject, process, and purpose. Kindergarten is a first step in enculturation, ensuring that all students share certain behaviors and attitudes, that in other words they all know the same things, and a PhD is a final step in differentiation, ensuring that each student is specialized enough to know something no one else knows.

In this forum our focus is specific, so I'd like to address the distinction between undergraduate and graduate education. My premise is that since each of us in this room is beginning graduate study, continuing graduate study, or overseeing graduate study, we would do well to be reflective about ways in which graduate study differs from undergraduate study. I don't expect in a ten-minute talk to give some exhaustive or definitive explication of the matter—I don't *have* a definitive explication—but I do hope to post a few provocations toward our further collective or individual reflection. My thesis is that undergraduate education is about (or ought to be about) *transformation*, and graduate education ought to be about *vocation*.

Though individual narratives differ, it would be typical of an undergraduate to have left circumstances of relatively thorough dependence on and regulation by external entities and entered circumstances of relatively thorough independence and self-regulation. In place of parents' provision of food and shelter, you earn scholarships and hold a job. And instead of parents setting curfew and police officers checking ID, *you* choose whether to go by yourself to the library to work derivatives and conjugate verbs, or to go with friends to a bar to see who can chug more Millers.

To meet those altered circumstances well demands personal transformation. The absence of economically and socially imposed authority creates a need for the means (and the will) to evaluate for yourself competing truth claims, to choose for yourself among competing value judgments, and so on. An ideal undergraduate education would offer the means for salubrious self-determination: economic independence and intellectual/moral/spiritual autonomy.

Typical circumstances for graduate students differ from typical circumstances for undergraduates. In most cases, graduate students are already "on their own," either by themselves or in chosen rather than given partnership. Some version, and some degree, of independence and autonomy have been won already. The *given* identity of childhood and youth has been transformed into a *chosen* identity. What is needed then is vocation. I don't mean by that a career: from my point of view the diminution of the concept of vocation into an economic category has a deadening effect on individual lives, a corrupting effect on educational institutions, and a stultifying effect on society. *Vocation* as I mean the word has nothing to do with how one makes a living. I mean *vocation* in its etymological sense, as calling.

If the transformation realized through undergraduate education manifests as independence and autonomy, the vocation realized through graduate education manifests as *inter*dependence and sustainability. What one needs in order to follow that which beckons one is, as with any odyssey, hospitality and sustenance. Each of us on the faculty interprets those needs differently, and seeks to meet them as she or he sees fit. For myself, I see my MFA teaching (as differentiated from my undergraduate teaching) as the tendering of sources and the modeling of practices. I'm persuaded that our community is as broad as humanity itself, and that the archives of the stories and ideas and songs of humanity are the hosts whose hospitality offers way stations as one follows the calling, as I am persuaded that the sustainability of a vocation of writing depends on its *practice.*

I doubt that, in commentary about the poem or essay or story on which you are working this week, I have anything to say that you will remember in ten years or that will resonate for you then. Truth be told, I suspect you'd be better off *defying* any commentary I offered than fulfilling it. I think I *can* point you to books, though, that you will read and re-read, books that will still matter to you in ten years, and in thirty. And I think I can read with you in those books in ways that we both will find sustaining, now and for the foreseeable future.

I once took a music history class at a Catholic college, and the professor, a nun, reminded us on the last day of class that her vocation was not teaching or music but prayer, and that though that particular class was over she would pray for us, her students, for the rest of her life. I have no gift for prayer, but on this first day of our academic year together I remind you that my vocation is not teaching or program direction. My vocation is writing, and if that gives me less to offer you than was offered me by the Sister, it does put me in league with you who share that vocation. Lyn Hejinian suggests that "Any characteristic act—whether it is a sailor's sailing or a hermit's withdrawal or a writer's writing—is an act of reciprocal invocation." *Invocation* shares the same root as *vocation*, so Hejinian's term seems as sound an ideal for a graduate education in writing as any I know, and I welcome you into, or back into, an MFA program that I hope fulfills that ideal by *being*, and by inviting each of us into, an ongoing act of reciprocal invocation.

4.

For the homiletic character of these remarks, I blame the occasion, our celebration through this forum of our annual re-formation as a purposive community. The occasion also lends my remarks, though, a feature I embrace without disclaimer, namely that they participate in this event's *welcoming*. Some of us—students and faculty—are returning from summers of intense reading, writing, travel, and thought, into our roles as contributors to the life of this community. To you (to us) I say, Welcome back. Others are entering this community for the first time. I am honored, as a speaker on this occasion, to represent the whole group in saying *WE* welcome you. We will seek constructive engagement with your urgencies as writers, citizens, and persons, and we look forward to your engagement with ours.

"Urgencies" may seem an odd word here, but I have reason for not saying we will engage with your "writing." We ought to remind ourselves occasionally how inadequate is the *name under which* we convene to the *basis on which* we labor together. The name "creative writing" misidentifies and misdescribes the work we share. In contrast to "literature," which names the object of study, "molecular biology," which names the field of study, or "law" or "business," which name the societal domain within which a practice occurs, "writing" names an activity. But even as synecdoche the term is misleading, because writing, though it is *one* activity we share, is *not* the most important one: *reading*, for example, and *attention* are both more definitive of our work. Better that you leave this program with shaky craft but a vital reading life and heightened attention, than with honed craft but a hollow reading life and attention that is not "dialed in"—with, in other words, nothing to sustain you. The "creative" part of "creative writing" is even more misleading than the "writing" part. "Creative" in ordinary usage suggests ungroundedness, irresponsibility, aimlessness, self-indulgence: we hold jobs in order to feed our families, we go to church to seek transcendent meaning and purpose, and on Saturday mornings in our spare hours we paint ceramic swans to be "creative." Against such a background, "creative writing" sounds flippant; it makes perfectly understandable, even inevitable, Robert Creeley's anecdote of having been asked once after a reading, "Was that a real poem or did you just make it up yourself?" The "creative" in our culture stands in contrast to, and offers respite from, the real.

But I want no respite from the real, and such respite would be unworthy as a purpose, for you or me individually or for us collectively. So in addressing the purpose of our purposive community, I venture such terms as our "work" and our "urgencies" on the grounds that they are, if not fully adequate, at least less trivializing than "creative writing." "Work" may look toward the *outcome* of our purposiveness and "urgencies" toward its *origin*, but my connecting them is neither new nor arbitrary: they are joined at the root. "Urgent" and "work" both derive from the Proto-Indo-European base, *werg-, the same base that gives us such other English words as "wreak," "organic," "ergonomic," and—my favorite—"orgy."

Using "urgencies" to refer to a set of otherwise disparate categories that share the feature of having purchase on us—obligations, longings, obsessions, questions, needs, hungers, accountabilities—I want to suggest that our work is construed most accurately and worthily not as "creative writing," but as the reconciliation, synthesis, and manifestation of urgencies through the vehicle of rational discourse. I mean by this something straightforward. An unhealthy or corrupt life can be explicated in terms of unreconciled urgencies. If I fulfill my declared commitment to the sacredness of human life by planning and committing the murder of abortion doctors, I have not satisfactorily reconciled my own urgencies, nor have I reconciled my urgencies with the urgencies of other persons. The reconciliation, synthesis, and manifestation of urgencies is a way in which those of you who do, and those of us who do not, profess the Christian religion may understand alike the imperative from Paul's Epistle to the Philippians to "work out your own salvation with fear and trembling." Nothing about the reconciliation of urgencies can be displaced onto others; it cannot be replaced simply by affiliation with a group or a cause; and nothing about it is given beforehand. No one can, and nothing will, reconcile or synthesize urgencies for you. In Walt Whitman's words, "Not I, not any one else can travel that road for you, / You must travel it for yourself." *This* is the sense in which writing is always already spiritual and political and moral: not that it speaks of Jesus or Shiva, or refers to Rwanda, or teaches a lesson, but that it pursues the regulatory ideals we designate with such terms as the religious term "transcendence," the political term "justice," and the moral term "virtue," ideals that stand in each of those domains for manifestly reconciled and synthesized urgencies.

In this sense, what we (so misleadingly) call "creative writing" epitomizes the form of discourse to which higher education has been committed from its origins in Plato's Academy, a form of discourse I will call "rational," though—let me emphasize—I don't mean by that only "logical." I mean a discourse the assumptions of which include: all humans are equally subject to (none exempt from) the limitations of methods of inquiry; the world's imperviousness to human subjugation is final; and (in principle and in practice alike) the attempt to adequate representation to reality is interminable. I mean by "rational" a discourse in which all humans are subject to, and none has special access to, what as a shorthand might be named "truth." So by rational discourse I do not mean only eristics or logic: a story or a jazz solo or a mystical vision or a mathematical proof or a lab experiment might well exemplify rational discourse. I do mean to contrast rational discourse with at least two other kinds of discourse, which I will call here "commercial" and "authoritarian." Commercial discourse eliminates equal standing before truth by dismissing truth as a criterion, and authoritarian discourse eliminates equal standing before truth by claiming special access to truth for one or for a few. Both corrupt communication. Commercial discourse corrupts communication by making its object the substitution of my interest for yours, and its means therefore the lie. Authoritarian discourse corrupts communication by making its object the equation of my will with the real, and its means therefore the command. Their corruption of communication would be enough by itself to oblige us to embrace rational discourse and resist commercial and authoritarian discourse, but the even more compelling reason is the regard each has for persons. Rational discourse envisions humans in the highest possible terms, as holding equal place within the real, and equal standing before the truth, and therefore as sharing common cause with one another, at all times and places, and under any conditions. Commercial discourse reduces humans to consumers, whose value is not inalienable but—just the opposite—fully externalized and fungible as the means of exchange. Authoritarian discourse divides humans into masters and slaves, whose value, far from being inalienable, is externalized as one's own power, or eliminated by the other's. Commercial and authoritarian discourse both attempt to consolidate agency in the hands of a few; rational discourse to distribute agency equally to all.

You see where I'm headed. We "creative writers" are not the only ones for whom the work is rational discourse, as Agnes Martin reminds us when she warns against thinking inspiration (her name for entry into what I am here calling rational discourse) "is reserved for a few," and Wislawa Szymborska when she declares that inspiration "is not the exclusive privilege of poets or artists." Our colleagues in other fields share in our work. Carlos Martinez del Rio in the Zoology and Physiology Department is immersed in rational discourse when he researches functional ecology; Teena Gabrielson in Political Science when she explicates concepts of citizenship; Bob Southard in the College of Law when he parses the rules of evidence; and the University President *ought* to be engaged in rational discourse in making and delivering the decisions upon which depends the functioning of this sodality of inquiry we call a university. We are by no means the only ones, but we are among those, for whom the work is rational discourse, and the stakes thus the fullness of our humanity and the humanity of others.

When I sit before a blank page or when you sit before a new word-processing document, our work is not the pursuit of fame and fortune, not self-expression, not creativity, not therapy, not publication, unless and exactly insofar as those further rational discourse. *Our work is to recognize and declare the equal standing of all persons before the truth.* A novel might do so by offering through its narrative a basis for identification with a character in whom the reader might not otherwise recognize common cause, a nonfiction piece might do so by documenting matters the neglect of which would give implicit sanction to continued withholding of agency from a person or a group, a poem might do so by revitalizing a metaphor that has been co-opted by commercial discourse. Regarding our work in this way might seem intimidating (I didn't ask to bear all humanity on my shoulders!), but it is also liberating. The work of self-expression, for instance, needs extrinsic validation, value added to it from another source to make it worthwhile for me or for others, but the work of rational discourse, the form of discourse that keeps alive the possibility that you and I might reconcile our urgencies rather than that one of us will subdue the other's urgencies to her or his own, has intrinsic value, needs no extrinsic validation, not even from its results. Even if Auden were right that "Poetry makes nothing happen," its being so would not diminish the value of literature, which is intrinsic, not contingent on any results it may occasion. In the terms of commercial or authoritarian discourse, no sound answer is available for such questions as "What good is an MFA?" or "What good is writing?", but in the terms of rational discourse the answer is given before the questions are asked. Similarly, regarding my work as rational discourse guides me in undertaking the work. Just as it liberates me from the need for extrinsic validation, by offering intrinsic (and therefore prior) value, so rational discourse relieves me of the need for external guidance, thus liberating me to purse intrinsic direction. I am bound only to make the work rational, not to satisfy the formulas of genre or the expectations of editors and agents and readers. The stakes are high—In what regard are we to hold humanity? How are my urgencies to be synthesized with one another and reconciled to the urgencies of others?—but they are the only stakes.

Engagement with this community I account one of the great privileges of my life, exceeded only by love for and from a generous and wise person, large of mind and heart. In such community members as Brad and Sam and Evie and Jeff and Beth

I find models for my life and writing, and from their intensities I draw sustenance. Since you also share now the privilege of participation in this community, I urge you—that word again—to work—*that* word again—as if your work were urgent, because it *is* urgent, because the realization—*that* word, "real," again—of the highest human ideals (trust, respect, rule of law, fair distribution of goods, equal distribution of justice, and so on) is conditioned by, and entirely dependent on, rational discourse. I do not mean here merely to assure you that our work matters; I mean to challenge you, to challenge *us*, to see our work at its weightiest, as the honoring and enactment of rational discourse, the reconciliation and synthesis of urgencies. I challenge us to regard our work as something that matters, yes, but also, without hyperbole, as the very work of higher education, even as the one human work, without which nothing else matters.

Take You a Course, Get You a Place

Art, all art, … is a foreign city, and we deceive ourselves when we think it familiar.

The woman beside me this morning
                    had a large freckle inside her left ear.
Not that we were intimate in the way
                    you might think first; merely near each other
in the crush at rush hour on the metro.
                    That she wore her hair pulled back revealed her ear.
Her dress signaled purpose: sleek glasses,
                    silk blouse, slender attaché. She seemed
not to notice me noticing her.
                    If, as I suspect, she rides to work
at this time each day, many before me
                    must have noticed this freckle. Like me,
others must have lost sight of it, and of her,
                    in the station, never to see it again.
    At the time the ear-freckled stranger and I
                    left that train, more people animated
the station we stepped into than live
                    in the town I call home. Maybe more
than in my *state*. I live in Laramie,
                    home of the only university
in the least populous state in the union,
                    Wyoming. The university
is halfway across town from my house,
                    so it takes me almost twenty minutes
to walk to work. I'm on a metro today
                    because UW has a faculty
exchange with Shanghai University,
                    so I'm here in China for three weeks,
to give six lectures on the subject
                    of American poetry. Of the two
substantives, "lecture" seems less to the point
                    than "exchange": immersion in this context

has highlighted my assumptions in
          such a way, and to such a degree,
that surely I am learning more about
          American poetry than my students are.
   My time here interrupts a writing project
          that has me reconsidering my
understanding of poetry and my ways
          of valuing it, but because my hosts
asked for recognizable figures
          —citing Robert Frost as their example—
I've structured things in a predictable,
          even retro, fashion: lecture one,
Whitman and Dickinson; two, the modernists;
          three, African-American poetry;
four, Frost; five, Bishop; six, contemporaries.
          Not the platonic form of poetry
in America, but a version
          I permit myself with the excuse that,
in fifteen hours of instructional time,
          no structure would be whole or perfect.
   I began the first lecture with a contrast.
          For all its changes in dynasties,
I observed (in a sweeping and surely
          indefensible generalization
that exhausted my knowledge of the matter),
          Chinese history has been continuous
in the sense that the majority
          in what we now know as the nation
of China would trace their lineage
          to peoples who occupied this same region
forty centuries ago or farther.
          U.S. history, in contrast, is defined,
I said, by a rupture, in which groups
          from another continent arrived
about five-hundred years ago, and displaced
          the peoples who had occupied the region

since the ice age. Soon enough, the newcomers
                    imported, in large numbers, persons
from yet *another* continent. So that
                    today the majority of citizens
in what we now call the U.S.A.
                    would trace their lineage to peoples
from across the sea. The fact of the rupture,
                    I asserted, leads the occupiers
to preoccupation with two problems:
                    to justify their claim to the land,
and to assert as independent
                    their identity in relation
to those who stayed on the continent
                    from which they came, or to those who stole them
from their continent of origin.
                    Keeping those preoccupations in mind,
I promised my patient auditors,
                    would help make sense of American verse.
    And indeed it does so. Even though
                    I'd been winging it—I'd prepared, yes,
a small anthology beforehand,
                    but my digest of world history
was just making up shit at the last minute—
                    seeing history through this observation
did highlight features I'd missed before
                    in poems with which I had thought myself
familiar. In that first lecture, then,
                    I began to see, for instance, Whitman's
love of the word "destined" as combining
                    both of the rationalizations
I had claimed that "we" urgently pursue,
                    as when, in "Thou Mother With Thy Equal Brood,"
he calls on the "Brain of the New World"
                    to "recast poems, churches, art," because
the Old World brain is dead, and "Its poems,
                    churches, arts, unwitting to themselves,

[were] destined with reference to thee."
                    So it is destiny that we fulfill
(and in fulfilling replace) the old world,
                    and destiny that we do so here,
that any impediments to our
                    poems, churches, and art be just that:
impediments, to be overcome
                    or, if need be, eradicated.
Impediments all, be they bison
                    or Pawnee, passenger pigeon or Sioux.
    My learning, though, was not to come from
                    my inventing undefended pronouncements
to apply to the poems; instead
                    it was to come from the starkness with which,
in so different a context, premises
                    that can stay tacit at home announce themselves.
This became clear early in the first lecture.
                    In my anthology, I had offered first
"The Chambered Nautilus," as a way
                    to show what Whitman and Dickinson
were reacting *against*. I pointed out
                    the regularity of meter,
in preparation for listening
                    to Whitman's more flexible metric.
The blank expressions of the students
                    alerted me to my own stupidity:
I was speaking of accentual meter
                    to an audience whose first language
is *tonal*. As difficult as it is
                    for me to hear the variations in tone
on which meaning in Mandarin is based,
                    so difficult must it be for them,
native speakers of Chinese, to hear
                    accentual meter in English.
So accustomed had I grown to arguing
                    that *regularity* of meter

is a faulty ideal, that I'd forgotten
             that meter's having *any* role at all
is accidental, not essential,
             wholly contingent on the language
in which a poem is composed, by no means
             necessary or universal.
    I have kept proposing dubious
             hypotheses. Of Frost, for instance,
I decided—on the bus to class—
             to declare him interested in *home*,
in having us look again at what feels
             familiar. I will contrast him, on this count,
to Bishop, calling him a public poet
             because his starting with the familiar
invites everyone in, and calling her
             a poet's poet because her starting
with the unfamiliar selects for her
             a smaller audience from the start.
Frost's poems, I declared for a verity,
             take us to a familiar place, but
orient us differently toward it.
             He situates his poems in New England
because that is "home" to America,
             the familiar place, in contrast to
the "frontier," the "wild west," which to this day
             stands for the strange and unfamiliar.
    I continue, though, to be brought up short.
             This afternoon's on Frost was my fifth lecture.
The students have shown the elaborate
             courtesy I had been led to expect:
at the end of each lecture, they applaud;
             they listen attentively, whether or not
I am making sense; and they hold questions
             for after class, never interrupting me.
Except once. Today, as we discussed
             (read: as I pontificated on)

"The Road Not Taken," I drew on the board
     a picture of a stick Frost standing
at a Y in the road. I explained
     that stick Frost knows nothing about what
is at the end of either road. In this way
     (I went on, growing more pompous and absurd),
stick Frost stands for all of us, at each
     decision point. We don't know if choosing
law school will make us rich, or film school
     make us famous. We decide based on
all-too-limited information,
     and must take what follows. So stick Frost knows
only that a lot of feet before his own
     have ventured one of the roads, few the other.
He follows the few. It was at this point
     that the prior strict decorum was breached.
A young woman raised her hand. I almost
     forgot to call on her, so surprised was I.
Her puzzlement showed on her face: "Why
     would he do that?" Good question, and one
to which any answer will make more sense
     if you have internalized a culture
that regards the frontier as a place
     of opportunity, inhabited by
an other who possesses none of the rights
     one must accord to those who inhabit home,
a culture accustomed to a concept
     of destiny that resembles Whitman's.
 Plenty for me to think about when
     I return to my writing project at home.
Meanwhile, between lectures I am seeing
     fragments of Shanghai. Though a visit
to the Yu Yuan a day or two ago
     has soured me on seeing what "ought" to be seen:
any sense of tranquility in that place
     has been overwhelmed by shops and vendors.

God keep me from amassing trinkets.
                    Of my trip to Shanghai, let me remember
not the Yu Yuan but that woman's freckle.
                    For my lectures I hope I shall be shriven,
as I hope to be provoked by their flaws
                    to reconsideration of their subject.

Is Not

A form is not imagination. A form brings out imagination.

Ninety-five Theses:
A Disputation on the Power and Efficacy
of the Formal in Poetry

1. I propose easeful death for the term "formal poetry."
2. As with "natural" in regard to ethical events, so with "formal" in regard to aesthetic objects: no definition of the term grounds valuation on the basis of it: an
   encompassing term, one that applies to all members of a set p, cannot distinguish
   one subset of p from another, much less establish the superiority of one subset
   over another.
3. Formal poetry? As opposed to what other kind?
4. First among the fallacies afforded by "formal poetry," tautology. Used to modify
   "poetry," "formal" adds no information. All poetry is formal. "Formal poetry" resembles "musical song" or "cruel torture."
5. Though the formal principles and devices employed in poetry be various (as the
   merest glance at any handbook to literature or encyclopedia of poetic terms would
   show) any poem, whatever particular principles it selects from that manifold, just
   is formal.
6. Because formality conditions poetry, participates in making poetry poetry, the
   term "formal" modifies "poetry" not with specification but as an honorific that
   tells more about the speaker's tastes than about the poetry in question.
7. To the list of fallacies that began with *tautology*, add *equivocation*. "Formal" has
   various meanings, such as "architectural" (in contrast to "organic," as in "a formal garden") and "mannered" (in contrast to "casual," as in "a formal reception").
   When advocates of a given body of poetry identify it *as* formal, distinguishing
   it from other poetry by its possession of some architectural characteristic (e.g.
   regular meter) that not all poetry possesses, but then validating the favored poetry
   by another meaning of "formal" (e.g. mannered), though it may not be distinctive
   in that regard, they equivocate by using one meaning of "formal" to tag certain
   poetry, and another to validate it, without concern for whether the poetry is vali-
   dated by the distinguishing meaning or distinguished by the validating meaning.
8. Does Yeats's "Coole Park, 1929" count as formal because of its versification, or
   for the courtesies it observes, as we speak of formality when one scrupulously
   observes courtesies in a social situation?
9. Does Josephine Miles' "Views from Gettysburg" count as formal for the loose
   regularity of its stanzas, or for the "official" quality leant it by the hallowed ground
   to which it refers?

10. Because "formal" has a range of meaning, each of us will recognize certain modes of formality but not others, in at least two senses of the term "recognize": only some modes but not others will I be able to identify and understand as formality, and only some will I elect to acknowledge and affirm as formality. The limits of the range of meaning I recognize for "formal" may address the limits of formality, but they follow from the limits of my understanding. An American visiting Japan, I am offered a business card: will I observe all the associated formalities?

11. My reluctance to acknowledge and affirm some modes of formality will be connected with formality's inextricability from social, communicative, and power relations. (For example, elaborate dedications, a peculiar version of formality once obligatory for books, hearken back to a different patronage system than holds today, one in which elaborate praise for patrons and deference to readers was good form. In a different system of patronage, a different formality holds, and today that older formality seems nostalgic or simply false.)

12. Formality, far from timeless and immutable, operates as language operates, and has diachronic and synchronic aspects just like language does.

13. Formality does not separate us from the world, cannot itself stand separate from the world.

14. John Dewey: "What is form in one connection is matter in another and vice-versa."

15. Fallacy watch: category mistake. When a president employs the term "axis of evil," the logical error arises through filling a conceptual category ("evil") by application of a criterion inadequate to the category (absence of active and explicit alliance with the U.S.). When poets or critics employ the term "formal poetry," they fill the category by some criterion inadequate to it, e.g., use of end rhyme and regular accentual meter.

16. Because all poetry is formal, *any* criterion would be inadequate to distinguish some poetry from other poetry as worthy of inclusion in the category "formal poetry."

17. The frequency with which they are equated with "formality" makes rhyme and meter the George W. and Jeb of poetry, accorded attention beyond their merits and granted authority to which their capacities are inadequate, with ill consequences for the body politic that elected them, and for the larger spheres across which their influence extends.

18. What virtues rhyme and meter possess do not fit them to govern form.

19. Any definition of "formal," used to subdivide poetry, will occasion inconsistency in application. Why count Hopkins' poems in "sprung rhythm" as "formal," but

label as "free" Muriel Rukeyser's litany "Waiting for Icarus," when neither follows a received metrical pattern, yet each abides by strict rules of construction? Why label Donald Justice's "Here in Katmandu" "formal" even though it employs neither rhyme nor meter, and "cheats" the received sestina pattern?

20. From category mistake follows false dilemma. As "axis of evil" reduces a complex range of moral and political stances and actions, amenable to varying valuations, to two value-settled categories, good and evil, so "formal poetry" creates by contrast a shadow category and reduces all poems to membership in one category or the other, despite the complex range of formal principles at work in poetry.

21. The term "formal poetry" pretends that divisions are clean, as in the presupposition that a poem either employs meter or does not. It would be more accurate to describe poems as operating along a continuum of relative regularity or irregularity of rhythmical patterning.

22. Recognizing some but not other vehicles of linguistic patterning as embodying "form" treats as a reality, and makes judgments on the basis of, a construct ("formal poetry") dependent on implicit contrast that cannot be made explicit, because the self-contradiction that inheres in the contrasting set ("non-formal poetry") makes it necessarily empty.

23. The false dilemma encourages choosing sides and talking past one another. We don't argue endlessly about whether one ought to be a sonnet writer or a villanelle writer, because we recognize that *as* a false dilemma. These theses aim to dye the false dilemma inherent in the term—let me not dignify it as a "concept"—"formal poetry."

24. To enforce a choice between them, categories must be exhaustive, mutually exclusive, and non-empty. I must choose between exercising and not exercising, but need not choose between tennis and mountain biking, because I might choose to do neither or to do both. I must choose between eating breakfast this morning and not doing so, but need not choose between eating breakfast and drinking coffee, because I might choose to do neither, or both. I must choose between writing poetry and not writing poetry, but *cannot* choose between writing formal poetry and writing non-formal poetry, any more than I can choose between writing poetry and breeding lampposts.

25. The perverse logic of the term "formal poetry" lends it a comical aspect that makes it seem hardly worth objecting to. Answering "what kind of poetry do you write" with "formal poetry" carries the punch-line, wiseass feel of answering "what kind of pet do you have" with "a living pet."

26. The obligation to contest the use of "formal poetry" would diminish if "formal

poetry" did not enact, in addition to its humorous aspect, a political aspect. Pro-
testations to the contrary notwithstanding, defining form as employment of
rhyme and meter is, at this time in this country with its literary and social history,
conservative and even reactionary. Like any form of signification, the valuations
implied by such definition extend into the political. Even well-wrought urns have
histories, as any museum curator can attest in these days of repatriation. Rhyme
and meter cannot elevate themselves, or poetry, above history and politics.

27. Slavoj Žižek: "*This very exclusion of something from the political is a political gesture
    par excellence.*"

28. Neglect of duration and intonation in favor of accent in meter privileges British
    over African influence on American speech. Treating accent as the real and valu-
    able in regard to rhythm in poetry, dismissing duration and intonation as "mere-
    ly" performative aspects of rhythm, sustains the status quo of academic and eco-
    nomic privilege, chooses—check out the recordings—Eliot's pendulous droning
    of "The Waste Land" over Brooks's hip-swung jazzing of "We Real Cool."

29. Charles Bernstein: "Style and form are as ideological as content and interpreta-
    tion."

30. Only attention trained too exclusively toward accent could have defended, as
    did one laurel-laden head a few years ago, the then predominantly white-male
    membership of the Board of Chancellors of the Academy of American Poets as
    resulting from valid, unbiased, purely aesthetic judgment.

31. Luce Irigaray: "As women, we have thus been enclosed in an order of forms inap-
    propriate to us. In order to exist, we must break out of these forms."

32. Form *as* politics. Form "does not just mean physical shape," Rosalind Krauss
    writes, but "refers to the imposition of distinctions on the indistinctness of cha-
    os—distinctions like inside/outside, figure/ground, male/female, living/dead."
    Form refers also to the transgression of such distinctions.

33. The analogy between "natural" and "formal" extends to other terms, such as "fac-
    tual." Taking fact according to Feuerbach's analysis as "that which from being an
    object of the intellect becomes a matter of conscience" suggests that "natural,"
    "true," "factual," and "formal" all name (each in its domain) points at which con-
    sent, from being voluntary and dialogical, becomes obligatory, coerced, enforced.

34. "Formal" fences a field that had only horizons.

35. As the burden of proof in regard to sexual preference lies with a claimant who
    would *exclude* one person from loving another, and in regard to race with a claim-
    ant who would limit validity to one range of the spectrum of skin colors, so the

burden of proof rests on the one who would restrict how form may manifest itself in poetry.

36. We all give ourselves up for something, and to something. If the two are the same, we name our loss *love*. If not, we name it *form*.

37. A girl is born into and raised by a tribe isolated from other civilizations. Her tribe's language, though functionally identical to English, arose independently, and its poetic tradition includes no record of or access to poetry from England, America, or other countries in which English is spoken. Her tribe prizes chiasmus above all other poetic devices. Poetry that skillfully deploys chiasmus is often chanted around the hearth, and collected in the textbooks assigned at her tribe's best universities and in the anthologies sold in its chain bookstores. She has learned to listen for chiasmus, and its pervasiveness in the tradition also makes chiasmus common to nearly all the poetry she admires, and by which she is moved. Her taste is not naïve, but is informed by her tribe's theorists, some of whom present chiasmus as an essential rather than an accidental feature of poetry, often by means of a natural law argument: chiasmus, they say, reflects the human life cycle, which ends where it began, in nonexistence. Chiastic poems alone merit the name "formal." When she attains her majority, the young woman, a prodigal sort, ventures out to see the world, and ends up at an American university, where she takes a British Lit survey course. She fails from sheer frustration, forced chiasmus-starved through sonnet after clunky, formless sonnet that begins in one place and ends in another. The young woman's professor views her preoccupation with chiasmus as arbitrary, and she herself sees her professor's preoccupation with rhyme and meter as arbitrary. Both assessments are correct, but she fails the course.

38. Nothing about rhyme and meter demands that we make them definitive of form, in preference to other devices, and nothing in either validates using them in this way.

39. Reduction of "formal" to "metered" and/or "rhymed" distorts the relative importance of meter and rhyme, elevating them unjustifiably beyond the many other elements of form. Why should the presence or absence of rhyme define a poem as formal, but not the presence or absence of, say, alliteration?

40. Why should only end rhyme make a poem "formal"? Why call a Robert Creeley poem free verse though it use internal rhyme, and a Molly Peacock poem formal when its end-rhymed lines are all enjambed?

41. Why deny the status of "form" to such manifestations of lexical or syntactic patterning as the seriality in Christopher Smart's *Jubilate Agno*?

42. Why is Thomas Hardy's placement of rhyming words at the ends of lines "formal," but not James Laughlin's imposition of line breaks according to syllabic patterns?

43. Marianne Moore's "The Steeple-Jack" bases its line divisions on syllable count, and each stanza repeats the order of line lengths, with the second and fifth line of each stanza bearing an end rhyme; each of Louis Zukofsky's "Eighty Flowers" determines its line length by word count; Elizabeth Bishop's "12 O'Clock News" employs marginal "titles" alongside prose paragraphs. Which is formal? Which is not?

44. I do *not* discourage the employment of rhyme and meter, only the use of "formal" to privilege their employment over the employment of other devices. The fault, dear Brutus, is not in the rhyme and meter, but in ourselves, in the importance and definitiveness certain of us attribute to them.

45. I do not contest *preference* for rhyme and meter over other formal devices, only the attribution of Kantian "objective universality" to that preference, and any consequent attempt to impose the preference on other readers and writers of poetry.

46. But if this is not about form itself, only about how we use the words "form" and "formal," why make such a fuss? I don't try to stop grocery stores from posting signs restricting express lanes to customers with "15 items or less," so why try to stop poets from employing the solecism "formal poetry"? Because the point extends beyond grammar: the term "formal poetry" perverts the conversation about form in poetry.

47. For the conversation about form to bear fruit, it needs a new perspective, a paradigm shift. The importance often assigned to rhyme and meter in contemporary discussion—their privileged status as criteria for "formal"—is contingent, not necessary. British poetry has long featured accentual meter and end rhyme, and some of us learned in sophomore survey to begin reading a poem by marking its meter and rhyme. But having taught ourselves since then—God rest our professors' New Critical souls—that British poetry never was the only poetry worth attending to, we would do well to broaden our formal attentions similarly.

48. I myself employ rhyme and meter often. A fair percentage of the poetry I read and have memorized employs rhyme and meter. Some of my best friends, as they say, use rhyme and meter. I do not, I reiterate, contest use of or taste for rhyme and meter, only the equating of them with form.

49. There is to tone-deafness a corresponding deficiency, form-deafness, from which one suffers who cannot hear form in Williams or Oppen.

50. Its being hard to specify does not prevent something's being a formal principle, as for instance in Dickinson's use of the dash. I could not say exactly what the formal

principle *is*, and she herself may not have been able to *state* the formal principle, but I recognize it *as* a formal principle, and she *applied* it successfully.

51. Its being concealed and going unnoticed by the reader does not negate form, either. I might never have recognized James Wright's "May Morning," presented on the page as a prose poem, as a sonnet, had not John D'Agata pointed it out.

52. Even its presenting itself as a non-principle does not prevent a principle's being a principle. "Low" speech, as in Shakespeare's comic characters, distinguishes itself from standard or elevated speech not only in diction but in such formal qualities as rhythm. The "prose" sentences in Juliana Spahr's *This Connection of Everyone with Lungs* add up to a rhythm that inheres in the whole though not in the parts.

53. Immanuel Kant: "[T]ranscendental law says … appearances must in mere intuition be subject to the formal conditions of space and time."

54. Rhyme and meter—two devices out of the broad range of tools, processes, and linguistic potentialities that may be employed in forming a poem—are formal; they are not form itself.

55. Rhyme and meter occur in the domain of form and participate in its polity, but (unlike time in Heidegger, or time and space in Kant) do not establish its boundaries, much less its horizon.

56. Philip Brady: "I don't mean a particular scheme, but an artistic arrangement of silences, spaces, and sounds. Form is the means whereby a poet embeds into a lyric moment the seed of immensity."

57. If *Leaves of Grass* does not seem formal, you're not listening.

58. Kierkegaard's Abraham understood that, though God might often, even usually, make ethical demands, a god who could only make ethical demands would not be God. Poetry may sometimes speak in rhyme and meter, but if it could speak *only* in rhyme and meter, it wouldn't be poetry.

59. Assertion of rhyme and meter as criteria or preconditions for poetry falls into presumption and irreverence, the aesthetic equivalent of that by which Browning's Johannes Agricola incriminates himself theologically. But (like the Hume of *Dialogues Concerning Natural Religion* or Socrates in conversation with Euthyphro) Browning's Caliban gives the corrective view: "You must not know His ways, and play Him off, / Sure of the issue." Johannes thinks he knows what God will do, must do. Caliban's deference toward Setebos offers a better model for an attitude toward poetry: "There may be something quiet o'er His head, / Out of His reach…. / This Quiet, all it hath a mind to, doth." Maybe poetry will follow preconditions we stipulate for it in advance. But maybe not.

60. Poetry now resembles church music in the time of Bach and Handel: institutionally supported (by the "old guard" of an institution in transition) because pop culture supports a more transparent, less "formal" medium (oratorio/mass vs. drama + opera; poetry vs. film + popular music).

61. Poetry, an activity of the gods it protests.

62. Rhyme and meter assume regularity as the regulative ideal. ("Regular" and "regulate" share a root.) But what of Frank Bidart's poetry, for instance, which seeks to mark with italicization, capitalization, and lineation a whole range of rhythm, pacing, accent, duration, intonation that pursues as its ideal not regularity but affinity to subject matter?

63. Poetry can march, but it can also dance.

64. George Steiner: "Each formal unit in the poem, the phoneme, the word, the grammatical bonds or elisions, the metrical arrangement, the stylistic conventions which attach it to other poems in the historical set or family, is charged with a semantic potential of innovation and inexhaustibility."

65. Poetry, fully and variously *in-formed*, seeks the maximal, not the minimal. It will not be restricted, and does not restrict itself, to only two devices of in-form-ation.

66. Enlarging the concept of form to include other elements on equal footing with rhyme and meter does not merely leave rhyme and meter undisturbed, passively allowing them to continue in the poem: it makes attention to them more active, more accurate, more acute. Not only is there more going on in a poem, Horatio, than rhyme and meter; there is more to rhyme and meter than attention to them alone discovers.

67. Meter acts in relation to other features of poetry, not in isolation. Like less regular rhythms, it combines with other sound elements to create expectations, which it then subverts or fulfils, according to the ambitions of the poem.

68. Regularity creates expectation. A first line in iambic pentameter suggests a second. But expectation lives between responsibility and resistance. Whether the second line is or is not in iambic pentameter indicates, not whether the poem is good or bad, formal or not formal, but which ideal—responsibility or resistance—the poem pursues with greater abandon.

69. *That* is the stakes for rhyme and meter. What are they, what are any formal devices, doing for the poem, if not orchestrating the hermeneutic circle, creating expectations that the poem may then fulfill or subvert, as other aspects such as tone and subject demand? In the fluency with which they manipulate expectations, not in the fact of their being rhyme and meter, lies their worth.

70. Overemphasis on rhyme and meter trivializes them, and *weakens* their effect. It makes a received form such as the sonnet into a crypt, bound to tradition, deprived of experimental and exploratory power, inclined too far toward preservation and too far away from destruction. It justifies the negative connotations of "closed" in the opposition open form/closed form.

71. We have a name for the poetry that most nearly fulfils the ideal of regularity in meter. We call it *doggerel.*

72. Rhyme and meter can serve as agents of discovery, the discovery that Joseph Brodsky thinks characterizes the poet, "for whom every word is not the end but the beginning of a thought; … who, having uttered *rai* ('paradise') or *tot svet* ('next world'), must mentally take the subsequent step of finding a rhyme for it. Thus *krai* ('edge/realm') and *otsvet* ('reflection') emerge, and the existence of those whose life has ended is prolonged."

73. Rhyme and meter are not alone in their aptitude for discovery. Peter Quartermain starts with other devices when he asserts the possibility of using a whole *range* of "language as agent of discovery: the puns, the handling of consonants, the variation of tempo and line…."

74. Is Millay's "If I should learn…" formal because it is a sonnet, or for its restraint and understatement, for what it leaves unsaid? Is H.D.'s "Fragment 113" formal because of its rhymes and off-rhymes, or for the deference it shows the original?

75. Valuing rhyme recognizes its power and potential, but valuing rhyme as if it alone among the features and devices of language created an utterance poetry is folly. The former enriches; the latter impoverishes.

76. If I elevate my diction, but do not break my utterance into lines, is that form? If I intentionally vary my syntax? If I make an allusion? Is any element or aspect of the poem *not* part of its form?

77. We want as readers and writers of poetry not to quarantine the "formal," but to set it in as broad and rich a context as possible. Tony Hoagland's warning against fashion might be issued also against "formal poetry": the danger, Hoagland says, is a "lack of perspective" that impedes recognition of "deep structure." Insofar as rhyme and meter matter, insofar as they lend poetry meaning or value, they do so because they embody deep structure.

78. A correlative from the moral realm: Kant's distinction between hypothetical and categorical. A hypothetical imperative might tend to bring good results, as we would likely say of the imperative to drive within the speed limit. But a hypothetical imperative carries no value in itself, and is subject to such corruptions

as hypocrisy. A hypothetical imperative carries virtue only insofar as it embodies a (*the*) categorical imperative. Similarly, a formal device such as rhyme might bring good results, but its ultimate aesthetic value derives from its embodying a deeper structure.

79. One such deeper structure is repetition and variation. Rhyme and meter are elements of form, but repetition and variation are *more* elemental. A Bach fugue demonstrates how even "pure" and "abstract" repetition/variation creates drama and nourishes emotion.

80. One might repeat end syllables (rhyme) or stress patterns (meter). But one might also repeat initial consonants (alliteration), grammatical structures, lines, words, rhetorical structures, etc. And one might vary any of those elements.

81. The basic question, for writers and readers of poetry, is how the elemental in poetry relates to the contextual. How, in other words, does it occur that a formal device such as rhyme may have psychological effects on an auditor or political effects on a socius? Can those effects be calculated? Can they be regulated? What are they? Are they good or bad? How does it come about that the syntax of a poem may suggest a metaphysical view? How is it possible that the diction in a poem can critique a government? Is the scope of such suggestion or critique enough to validate the labor of writing the poem? Is the nothing that poetry makes happen the nothing that is not there or the nothing that is?

82. That basic question can be formulated in this way: why does poetry, which appears to be determined by its *internal* conditions, have (external) *effects*, on individual readers, on the broader communities in which it finds an audience, and so on? Form looks like a game, but it has *consequences*.

83. Asked specifically by a poet, the question takes a pragmatic turn: how do I employ the elements (what I can control) to create effects (what I can't control), such that those effects realize some value term (progressive, beautiful, edifying…)?

84. Like telescopes or microscopes, poems are a technology that furthers our ability to perceive and understand reality. Like a telescope they distort reality, but like a telescope they alert us that reality is distorted, that we are seeing *through* a technological device. (Cynthia Macdonald: "seers recognize their visions as distinct from other seeing.") We learn how to contextualize that viewing, how to compensate for it, how to *read* it. That it selects and distorts the reality we see through it does not prevent the telescope from showing us something true about the world that we couldn't have learned without the instrument. So with formal devices, the "lenses" of the poem.

85. Hart Crane: "The poet's concern must be, as always, self-discipline toward a formal integration of experience."

86. Form mediates between whatever causes (social circumstances, authorial intention, etc.) may stand at the origin of the poem and whatever effects the poem may have. Form mediates between writer and reader, between the creation of the poem and its reception.

87. The conversation about form has value when it reorients us toward, and returns us to, the basic question. The conversation is trivial when it creates identification rather than rumination. At the risk of tedium, a restatement of my claim: application of the term "formal poetry" trivializes the conversation about form, diverts it from the basic question. And a reiteration of my disclaimer: these theses do not seek immediate influence on the practice of form. They do not urge poets toward or away from particular formal approaches, such as emphasis on rhyme and meter. They address the conversation about form, and urge reorientation of that conversation.

88. Rhyme and meter encode inclination toward regularity of pattern, simplicity, fulfillment of expectation.

89. Meter, regarded as accent or stress, offers only a thin account of the rhythmical aspect of poetry. Accent leaves out pitch, timbre, pacing, volume, tone, inflection. Its being easy to mark does not make accent more real or more important than rhythmic features that may be less susceptible to notation.

90. The need for a more robust account of rhythm can be illustrated simply. The sentence "I can hardly wait" has the accentual pattern heavy light heavy light heavy. But without varying that accentual pattern, one can make the sentence bear opposite meanings. By drawing out the duration of the last syllable and by raising one's pitch in pronouncing it, one can make the sentence mean I am eagerly waiting. But by drawing out the duration of "hard" and compressing the duration of "wait," combined with lowering one's pitch for the last three syllables, one can make the sentence mean I am waiting with dread.

91. Rather than trying to characterize some poetry as "formal" and distinguish it from other poetry, a more interesting and more fruitful approach (perhaps more interesting *because* more fruitful) would inquire into the whole range of what Gerald Bruns calls "enabling conditions" that make a poem a poem, what those conditions are and how they enable.

92. It is not some element or pair of elements that in-forms the poem. It is the *combination* of elements, and the dynamic interactions between them.

93. Pattern can be simple or complex, and either can yield beauty. An Agnes Martin

painting finds beauty in simple geometry. A fractal such as a fern leaf makes beauty of a more complex geometry. Accentual meter seeks the simple, but the simple is not the only possibility for form. Our world is enriched by Agnes Martin paintings and would be impoverished by their absence, but so is it enriched by ferns.

94. The formal confined to rhyme and meter resembles the physical confined to Newtonian mechanics: it explains a lot, but also gets the universe wrong.

95. Names can reveal; names can obscure. Some religions impose a taboo against speaking the name of the divinity, recognizing such speaking as blasphemous. In a kind of aesthetic parallel, the term "formal poetry," inadequate to its object, *mis*names even as it names, defends us against what it seeks to name. "The Tao that can be named is not the eternal Tao." We would be more reverent toward what we (seek to) revere, would better approximate an absolute relation to the absolute we seek, if we would absent ourselves a while from application of the falsifying formula "formal poetry."

If Design Govern

Though a matter involve matter, matter may not matter most.
A wave may be made of water, but also travels
through it. *Travels through*, in fact, more than *is made*
of. The water stays in place; only the wave moves.

So here. In all I have said I have sought
to say that we understand the body's hungers by the
spirit's, not the other way around. Hunger names the spirit's
need for nourishment literally, but names the body's only metaphorically.

The sonnet speaks of the body's hungers, surely, but of
the spirit's more. So I seek to speak when I
speak of sonnets. As I seek to know when I
know my beloved. Her body, yes, let me touch attentively
that locus of my longing, spring that ever offers also
and more. As does the sonnet. As may I here.

1.   (Robert Frost, "Design")

If Donne merits the designation "metaphysical," so does the sonnet.
Grant to Wittgenstein that in metaphysics "the difference between factual
and conceptual investigations is not clear to it. A metaphysical
question is always in appearance a factual one, although the
problem is a conceptual one." Grant that "like everything metaphysical
the harmony between thought and reality is to be found
in the grammar of the language." Then let the sonnet
stand as one grammar in which the metaphysical manifests itself.

Make thus the metaphysic in Frost's "Design" less theological than
grammatical, its assertion ("I found a dimpled spider"), its questions
("What had that flower to do with being white"), and
its hypothetical ("If design govern in a thing so small")
attuned to reality, and reality to them, because—and only
because—they themselves constitute a small thing governed by design.

2.   (Christian Wiman, "Revenant")

"I did not bid you tell me one or two
of the many pious actions but that form itself that
makes all pious actions pious." If the sonnet *does* stand
as one grammar in which the metaphysical manifests itself, we
may cite examples, but must also seek essence, looking not
first for markers (fourteen lines, iambic pentameter), but for features
(ratio, turn, accretion, experiment, tension and release) that in-form, grace,
bestow essence, and fever the air, sparking spirits into speech.

Not necessarily expecting to find them. Essence, if essence there
be, may not show up in the shared, so, like
Christian Wiman's revenant, we may love storms because they are
not ours. We may die "braced alone in the breaking
heat," having waited in vain "to feel the burn that
never came: / that furious insight and the end of pain."

3.   (John Donne, "Holy Sonnet 7")

The 8:6 ratio of lines in a standard sonnet—octave
and sestet—matches the ratio of the length of the
shorter sides of the paradigmatic Pythagorean right triangle. As in
right triangles, where the hypotenuse reclines, the longest side, so
in sonnets that which joins the far ends of octave
and sestet back to one another, creating a whole, must
be longest. Four joined to three and governed by design
necessitates something greater than either, in geometric or poetic figure.

In Donne's seventh "Holy Sonnet," the octave calls on angels
to blow their trumpets so the "numberless infinities of souls"
may rise. The sestet, though, calls on Jesus himself to
do something contrary: "let them sleep, Lord." Those imperatives—hurry
(octave), wait (sestet)—find connection through the paradoxical relationship of
humans to the good. We must repent, we need grace.

4.   **(Gerard Manley Hopkins, "God's Grandeur")**

What to name that excess by which ratio exceeds sum,
if not grace? Hopkins, calling it "the grandeur of God,"
insists that with it "the world is charged": electrically charged
("like shining from shook foil"), and charged as in commanded
(we ought to "reck his rod"). There is a sum,
called nature, "never spent," as there is octave and sestet
in the sonnet, that shows itself in "the last lights
off the black West" and "morning at the brown brink."

But world and sonnet both host a whole that exceeds
sum, beyond what our "foot feel," not things themselves but
"the dearest freshness deep down" them, there because, in Hopkins'
terminology and tradition, "the Holy Ghost over the bent / World
broods"—yes, *broods:* grace also names the inseparability of grief
and love—"with warm breast and with ah! bright wings."

5.   **(John Keats, "Bright Star…")**

It, whatever it is that no name names, gets *named at*
by rationality and ratiocination, those pursuits of ratio, the aspect
of the universe we humans can access, the ass with
which the god who made the blinding sun mooned Moses.
Meno's slave boy spoke Greek because he'd been taught in
Meno's house, but what he knew before his father's irrational
urges overflowed into his mother was ratio, that twice two
equals four, that a double figure grows from the diagonal.

And Keats knew what? To gaze "on the new soft-fallen
mask / Of snow upon the mountains and the moors," to
seek the "soft swell and fall" of his "fair love's
ripening breast," to stay "Still, still" for "her tender-taken breath."
To give eight lines to the star, six to the
lover, and so reserve fourteen for his splendid short-lived self.

6. (Louise Bogan, "Morning")

Different ratios seek different ends. One sum hosts many ratios.
7:7, leaning as it does against the sonnet's standard 8:6,
brings balance into question. But the same ratio from a
different sum, a number standing on its own without the
sonnet's norm to shade it, reads differently. Louise Bogan's "Morning"
arrives in paired terms: eggs and breast, convolvulus and rose.
Like the colors with which it starts, the five-line stanzas

complement one another, no question of imbalance haunting the poem.
In another poem, dissonance with normal sonnet form might act
like half-mad Hamlet holding up the mirror to Gertrude in
her closet, projecting his questions finally onto the reader. In
"Morning," symmetry unshadowed by the sonnet's ratio insulates the reader,
keeps distant the disturbing question: is it sight or instinct
"That calls back these birds, to cherish and to guard"?

7. (Donald Hall, "Names of Horses")

Still, ratio, not number per se, seeds sense and song.
The sonnet selects eight and six, but a similar rise
and fall sounds through any numbers in the same ratio.
So even though Donald Hall doubles the numbers, the ratio
stays. Four four-line stanzas depict the horses' lives, pulling sledges
of cordwood, cartloads of manure, the mowing machine, the "clawed
rake," the hayrack, and a "leather quartertop buggy," their necks
all the while smoothing the wood of the stall's sill.

Three stanzas then describe the horses' deaths, how the time
came when "the man who fed you and kept you…
fired the slug into your brain, and felled you into
your grave." Even the last line, the list of names,
reiterates the ratio it trusts: seven names, four and three;
in the last three names, seven syllables, four and three.

8.   **(William Wordsworth, "The World Is Too Much With Us")**

Mathematicians and musicians tell us harmony arises out of ratio.
A pitch, always also a wavelength, can be named or
numbered, and any interval heard can be measured also. Attunement
can be standardized—has been standardized, to A440, to the
well-tempered scale. Human individuals and human societies, however, sometimes become
(or, more likely, always are) intemperate, a fact that demands
expression, and any expression of which calls for some unhinging
of pitch, some questioning of standards, some disturbance of ratio.

When "the world is too much with us," when "for
everything, we are out of tune," octave and sestet should
show the fact, so Wordsworth's "It moves us not," connected
grammatically back to octave but by lineation with sestet, disturbs
the 8:6 that might better suit, had we not "given
our hearts away," did our glimpses make us "less forlorn."

9.   **(John Milton, "On His Blindness")**

The sonnet waits as we wait when we wait well,
attentively. Occupied, the sonnet is an occupation. Given, chosen, earned,
enforced, all four. Ortega says that the "occupations, to which
we dedicate our lives, do not come as imposed upon
us." Milton's Patience, that "God doth not need / Either man's
work or his own gifts," and "who best / Bear his
mild yoke, they serve him best." Occupation can be borne
well or poorly, come how and from whom it may.

Something metaphysical gets staked, then, something is evoked in us,
when ratio holds its six until after its eight. More
Ortega: "He who waits... is making time *for* something, but
he who simply lets time pass is losing time—unmaking
it." Thoreau: "As if you could kill time without injuring
eternity." Milton: "They also serve who only stand and wait."

10.   **(Annie Finch, "No Snake")**

If a poem be Eden, we start inside, seeking the
snake that may be there or not, wanting belief, obedience,
ruin, all at once, since they go together better than
father, son, and holy spirit, or reason, virtue, and happiness.

Antonio Porchia: "Suffering is above, not below. And everyone thinks
that suffering is below. And everyone wants to rise." Into
solitude and love, two more inseparables, two more searchings-out, lookings-down.

4:3:4:3 instead of 8:6 means split in more ways than
one, means out of, means memory rhymes with free, yes,
though a growing shadow separates them. Ratio holds, but ratio
rises out of fragment, so it's "made again of memory."

Out of implies into, though sometimes as a counterfactual, sometimes
marking in the same gesture its absence. If a poem
be Eden, we return to it believing in dark heights.

11.   **(Robert Frost, "The Flood")**

Brad Leithauser finds conventional prosody "constructed by 'evenness': iambs, couplets,
quatrains, octets, the sonnet's bipartite assertion and rejoinder." Not surprising,
since, after the first evenness, all prime numbers are odd;
even numbers added together always create more even numbers, but
an even number of odd numbers added together yields an
even number. And so on. Even seems simply more ordered
than does odd, Plato's *Laws* be damned, so where order
purports to be essential, as in poetry, evenness seems obligatory.

But oddness, like disorder, "has been harder to dam back
than water," so Frost's "The Flood" presents a flood of
syllables in its bloody octet, which spills over with eighty-eight
syllables, averaging eleven syllables per line instead of ten, leaving
the even lines in the sixty-syllabled sestet to feel like
the post-flood tatters his "Directive" hangs "on barb and thorn."

12.   **(Michael Burns, "Farm Road 93")**

As ratio stands to logos, so stands turn to mythos.
Turn, occurring often but not always at the transition from
octave to sestet, functions as a narrative feature of the
sonnet, its dramatic axis. We say "turn of events," but
in a sonnet nearly anything may turn. In Michael Burns's
"Farm Road 93," not events per se, but rather modality,
the relation of speaker to events, turns, from *is* to
might be, or in Aristotle's terms from history to philosophy.

The octave's actualities about the world ("my pickup wants to
skate / down every hill"), the speaker's life, other people, and
the speaker's internal state ("mild regret") turn into the sestet's
possibilities about what I might be able to do ("watch
the ducks") and make believe (that "I'm talking to God"),
motivating re-turn, through resolution: "I'm taking the long way back."

13.   **(Gwendolyn Brooks, "still do I keep my look…")**

No turn could anchor human narrative more inexorably than the
turn Gwendolyn Brooks builds into "still do I keep my
look, my identity…," the turn from life to death. After
starting in life, alleging the body's ability to retain through
all of life's vicissitudes (passion, pain, grief, hatred, wealth, poverty,
"good, nothing, or ill") its own unique "pose," which carries
with it value (it is "precious") and necessity (it is
"prescribed"), the poem turns itself, and turns us, toward death,

but it reverses the standard (Platonic, Christian) view that the
perdurable soul perpetuates identity beyond the hasty end of the
fugitive body, positing instead the *body* as the form of
continuity. Even in death, Brooks asserts, a human body remains
"like no other," and shows "the old personal art," shows
"what / It showed at baseball. What it showed at school."

14.   **(Quan Barry, "Asylum")**

Dewey: In "two sorts of possible worlds" no esthetic experience
would occur. "In a world of mere flux, change would
not be cumulative; it would not move toward a close."
Similarly, "a world that is finished, ended, would have no
traits of suspense and crisis, and would offer no opportunity
for resolution." The moment "of passage from disturbance into harmony"
grants "intensest life." The greatest dynamism, Dewey tells us, generates
the greatest aesthetic interest and bears the most existential weight.

As, for example, when nature begins patiently restoring a place
left almost barren by another act in our yet unconsummated
human effort toward self-destruction. "The fish are the first to
return," Barry says, then the sea turtles, then the birds
and the flowers, "all drawn to what we desert, a
preserve / where the chinese lantern's elliptic seed / is bone-smooth, cesium-laced."

15.   **(Edna St. Vincent Millay, "If I Should Learn")**

Turn in a sonnet has a double manifestation, a double
life: formal life as the transition from octave to sestet,
and logical, rhetorical life. Formally, the turn may rest neatly
at the juncture between octave and sestet, or may strain
more restlessly against such normalcy. The logic may announce itself
plainly or be more secretive. An instance of the former
occurs in Edna St. Vincent Millay's "If I Should Learn,"
where the poem embodies a hypothetical: if x then y.

"If I should learn," the speaker says (suffering in advance,
and saying now what she knows she will not be
able to show then), "That you were gone, not to
return again," then "I should not cry aloud," but instead
disclose my altered inner state by watching "the station lights
rush by / With a more careful interest on my face."

16.   **(Jennifer Atkinson, "March Snow")**

A sonnet's turn may mimic its subject as readily as
it may manifest any other logic. Like one season's transition
to the next, Jennifer Atkinson's "March Snow" hesitates at its
turn: it begins in "the ice-grizzled hemlocks," among which the
speaker walks "till dusk," before turning to the snow, to
"the regular tick / Of its falling," then deciding at last
to return to the human world that hosts *our* window,
at which, validating her decision, the snow is "already rain."

By invoking (and questioning) Socrates, obviously, but also Howard Nemerov's
little meditation "Because You Asked about the Line between Prose
and Poetry," in which the opposite turn occurs, from "silver
aslant" to "a moment that you couldn't tell" to when
"they clearly flew instead of fell," Atkinson layers meanings (logics,
rhetorics) onto one another like, well, snow layered over snow.

17.   **(Kathleen Peirce, "Dreaming of Sleep")**

A turn's being literal does not make it real, nor
does its being metaphorical make a turn unreal. Nothing could
cause more hurt than that the dream of *reality*, the
dream, put another way, of being able to understand and
justify and communicate experience, the dream that experience could be,
even potentially, shared, can manifest itself only in contradiction to
itself, as the *dream* of reality, and therefore (though experienceable,
though it be experience itself) by definition unjustifiable and incommunicable.

That the dream be always turning may afford a clue
that the turn fulfils the hermetic function, moving between the
two worlds, revealing and concealing, revealing as concealment, and concealing
as revelation, "a room in red which held / the one
bed and a window, where we looked away, blurred / as
if two books at once were being read to us."

18.   (Natasha Trethewey, "(Self) Portrait")

Between a poetry of opinion and a poetry of ideas
gapes a great gulf. The former takes dictation, then brings
down its stone tablets from the mountain; the latter limps
from wounds suffered in its agons with angels. Ideas, as
Plato intimated, seldom express themselves as themselves. Instead, they haunt
experience, buried several layers under it, as they haunt Ophelia,
the speaker in Natasha Trethewey's "(Self) Portrait," the way she,
the photographer's subject, finds herself buried under her own photographs.

Imagined by Trethewey from photographs by E. J. Bellocq, Ophelia
in the poem is shown—ironically—trying to imagine herself
instead of being imagined exclusively by others, placing herself on
the other side of the objectifying camera, and finding, when
she "looked into / a capped lens," herself, "my own clear
eye," there under the layers of imagination, where ideas float.

19.   (Leslie Scalapino, "Let me explain…")

Leslie Scalapino asserts that "individuals in writing or speaking may
create a different syntax to articulate experience, as that is
the only way experience occurs." For *may* I read *must*.
Someone else's syntax, someone else's experience. One's life is not
automatically one's own, not automatically a life. "Let me explain
what I mean by thinking about a man" in such
a way that my experi-*ment* in syntax creates the conditions
for the possibility of my having an experi-*ence*. Any experience.

"I undress him simply by thinking about the way he
walks / as being the way a baboon walks…" Nothing magical
about creating conditions for the possibility of experience, "simply" essential.
Without scarred syntax, experience withholds itself from us. Simply. Unconditionally.
"So far, the idea of the dog's bark is sim- /
ply the way I have found to describe a man's sounds."

20.   **(Elizabeth Barrett Browning, "Sonnets from the Portuguese" 6)**

Examining such of the sonnet's features as ratio and turn
naturally overstates their clarity and constancy. Other features challenge them—
blur and stretch them—and one such feature is accumulation,
which for instance can push the turn from its "natural"
place between octave and sestet to the end or the
beginning of the poem, even as early as the fourth
word. "Go from me. Yet…" begins Elizabeth Barrett Browning. Leaving
the poem, having turned, to accumulate qualifications to the imperative.

Yet "I shall stand / Henceforward in thy shadow," my volition—
my soul—no longer my own, my pleasure in the
world always qualified by "that which I forbore,… / Thy touch
upon the palm." I carry you in my emotions, my
actions, my dreams, my prayers; in my physical, mental, and
spiritual life. Even God no longer can tell us apart.

21.   **(Robert Browning, "Sonnet")**

If Elizabeth can turn four words from the beginning, Robert
can turn four words from the end, accumulating before the
turn instead of after it. "Eyes, calm beside thee… / May
turn away thick with fast gathering tears," he begins, as
if to echo her ending (though *only* as if—this
is an early poem). Then comes the accumulation of information:
others whisper "passionate praises" of you; others' blushes signal you,
your own blushes reply; "Their accents linger" in your ears.

You recall me only as a "still, guarded, very pale"
figure. The accumulated signals lead you to infer that "O'er
them all" except me your "beauty… did prevail," but the
turn reveals that the accumulation is incomplete, and the signals
therefore misleading: "Lady couldst thou know!" The sonnet's features (e.g.,
ratio, turn, accumulation) alter, but also depend on, one another.

22.   (William Shakespeare, "Sonnet 130")

Accumulation lends itself to qualification: I affirm one thing, yet
I recognize another. Perhaps the most obvious example of such
a "yes, but" occurs in Shakespeare's "Sonnet 130," which takes
at face value neither the mistress nor the troubadour tradition
of extravagant praise. "To His Coy Mistress" forfeits praise of
the mistress' various body parts out of haste: I'd have
spent "An hundred years" praising your eyes, "Two hundred to
adore each breast," and so on, but we're both dying.

"Sonnet 130" forfeits praise for more modest reasons, a preference
for understatement over hyperbole, combined with the same impulse as
Bonnie Raitt's sage imperative, "don't advertise your man." My mistress'
eyes ain't bright; her lips ain't red; her breasts ain't
white; etc. Faint praise saved by the inevitable "And yet,"
that she is more "rare" than other, more alluring mistresses.

23.   (Countee Cullen, "Yet Do I Marvel")

The converse of a "yes…but" sonnet of praise such as
Shakespeare's would be a "yes…but" sonnet of complaint such as
Cullen's "Yet Do I Marvel," in which assertions of God's
transcendence accumulate, from items transparent to humans ("I doubt not
God is good, well-meaning, kind") through those that need rather
more explanation (the sufferings of Tantalus and Sisyphus) to those
too complex for human comprehension ("Inscrutable His ways are"; it's
hard to "understand / What awful brain compels His awful hand").

Accumulation pushes turn to the final couplet: "Yet do I
marvel at this curious thing: / To make a poet black,
and bid him sing!" Though for a race rather than
for an individual, and though not accompanied by a petition
("Mine, O thou lord of life, send my roots rain"),
Cullen's complaint compares otherwise with Hopkins' "Thou art indeed just…."

24.   (Claude McKay, "The Harlem Dancer")

That in Cullen the turn gets pushed to the couplet
may be a cue that Petrarchan sonnets emphasize turn, and
Shakespearean, accumulation. Which must mean that in the sonnet ratio
knows more variation than these dispensings so far have rationed,
and that ratio results from, and varies according to, turn
and accumulation. In those terms, which would make of "Yet
Do I Marvel" a 4:4:4:2 subset of the standard 8:6,
McKay's "Harlem Dancer" looks like 12:2, a different ratio altogether.

The twelve lines of the quatrains accumulate details of the
interactions between the dancer and her audience: applauding, laughing, singing,
dancing, drinking, tossing of coins, and even "devouring." The couplet
then alters everything, stating the speaker's inference from the experience,
but also withdrawing dancer and reader alike from the scene:
"I knew her self was not in that strange place."

25.   (Christopher Smart, *Jubilate Agno*)

A true etymology: L. *experimentum*, from *experiri*, to try. Same
root as experience, expert, expertise. Now a false etymology: ex+peri+ment,
from L. *mens*, mind. To take one's mind out and
around. Both the true etymology and the false etymology say something
useful about experiment. Together, they identify it as a trying,
an essaying that rises from, that helps to create and
define, experience; and equally as a taking of one's mind
out beyond its place of rest, compelling it to wander.

As Christopher Smart tries in his experience-modifying way, urging a
wandering of the mind in the fourteen lines of *Jubilate
Agno* (584-597) beginning "For the spiritual musick is as follows,"
and then essaying to project the tones of musical instruments
onto particular rhymes in English, because "every word has its
marrow in the English tongue for order and for delight."

26.   **(Walt Whitman, "Thou Mother With Thy Equal Brood")**

Applied to poetry, "experimental," far from naming a clearly bounded
corpus, identifies instead an attitude, a stance that sees form
not primarily as restricting and ordering but as generating and
prompting, as drawing one into unexplored territory; less as our
connection with tradition than as our guide to the future,
the possible. Experiment thinks as the "Brain of the New
World" that Whitman tasked "to recast poems, churches, art," to
formulate the modern from "the background of the mighty past."

Not that future and past are independent. The future "lay
folded like an unborn babe" within the past, "carefully prepared
by it"; now the future unfolds and matures the past,
"the essence of the by-gone time contained" in it. If
the sonnet consists of repetition with variation, then tradition provides
repetition and experiment provides variation, each essential to the other.

27.   **(Francis Petrarch, 102; Sir Thomas Wyatt IX)**

The sonnet in English maintained from the start an attitude
of experiment. Rebholz: Petrarch "was Wyatt's primary model and inspiration"
in the sonnet, but Wyatt's sonnets do "not so consistently
as Petrarch's" employ "an important break after the eighth line,"
and they typically follow a different rhyme scheme, ending the
sestet in a couplet. Petrarch's "Però, s' alcuna volta i'
rido o canto, / Faccio 'l perch' i' non ho se
non quest'una / Via da celare il mio angoscioso pianto" becomes
Wyatt's "Whereby if I laughed any time or season, / It
is for because I have n'other way / To cloak my
care but under sport and play." Wyatt *adopted* a form,
certainly, but *modified* the form he adopted. We now view
his poems as traditional, but he wrote them as experiments.
They violated as much as they obeyed the received form.

28.   **(William Shakespeare, "Sonnet 73")**

The history of form is a dynamic, a tension between
experiment and tradition. Experiment ventures something new; successful experiments then
through acceptance and imitation become traditional form, which prompts resistance
(experiment), some results of which become tradition, and so on.

Once Wyatt had imported Petrarch and introduced the concluding couplet,
Shakespeare could follow suit, but also go Wyatt one better:
instead of an octave joined to a sestet that rises
to a couplet, four distinct quatrains capped by a couplet.

Which he employs to particularly powerful effect in the rightfully
famous 73rd sonnet, in which the speaker, addressing a younger
lover, laments his own advancing age, employing three related metaphors,
one per quatrain: I'm autumn, I'm twilight, and I'm a

fire's dying embers. Leaving the couplet to implore the lover
to "love that well which thou must leave ere long."

29.   **(W. B. Yeats, "Never Give All the Heart")**

Or consider Yeats's advice against giving oneself fully, "for love /
Will hardly seem worth thinking of / To passionate women if
it seem / Certain." Another experiment, this time with rhyme scheme
and line grouping (it is *all* in couplets, rather than
in quatrains that lead to a couplet), but also with
line length, choosing tetrameter over pentameter, in keeping with its
own assertion that "everything that's lovely is / But a brief,
dreamy, kind delight," making yet another land-grab for the sonnet.

Were tradition fixed and static, experiment would have to dismiss
it (staking ground outside of it) or diminish it (claiming
ground from it). But tradition's boundaries are *not* fixed, so
new land can be claimed *for* it, not only *from*
it. Experiment neither wounds nor undercuts but *expands* tradition, adding
more land for its heirs to plow—or to wander.

30.   (Brad Leithauser, "Post-Coitum Tristesse")

Experiment with rhyme scheme need not confine itself to altering
the order of the rhymes. In "Post-Coitum Tristesse: A Sonnet,"
Brad Leithauser leaves the rhymes in a "normal" order, abbacddceeeeeff
(or eeeee); the experiment is that there are *only* rhymes.
The whole poem, with line breaks eliminated, (each word is
its own line, and "hum-drum" is two) goes: "Why do
you sigh, roar, fall, all for some hum-drum come—mm?
Hm…" Which makes this poem also an experiment with meter,
since the individual lines (the whole poem is not much
longer than a "normal" line in a sonnet) can hardly
be said to have meter at all. And makes the
poem a good counterexample to the common assumptions that experiment
implies a *loosening* of constraints—it might mean a *tightening*
of them—and that experimentation happens only in free verse.

31.   (Marilyn Nelson, "Chopin")

If Wyatt, a Brit, can make an Italian tradition his
own, so can Marilyn Nelson, an African-American, make an Anglo-American
tradition her own: "Why don't we instead take possession of,
why don't we own, the tradition? Own the masters, all
of them." As African-American poetry always has done, and Nelson's
"Chopin" does, showing that such ownership need not be blind:
in the poem, an educated Black man reads receipts from
illiterate neighbors "and shows which white store cheats / these patrons."

John Dewey: "Great original artists take a tradition into themselves.
They have not shunned but digested it. Then the very
conflict set up between it and what is new in
themselves and in their environment creates the tension that demands
a new mode of expression." Experiment occurs when one tradition
gets incorporated into a life already assembled from other traditions.

32.   **(Czeslaw Milosz, "A Felicitous Life")**

"Every dynamic component of form . . . has within itself the restlessness
to exceed itself. . . . The restlessness of a line: it wants
to be a plane. The restlessness of a plane: it
wants to be space." If what Heinz Mack asserts of
visual art holds also for poetry, then experiment is art's
original sin ("Our hearts are restless until they find rest
in Thee"), but also what advances art, gives it dimension,
makes it felicitous, and connects it per aspera ad astra.

So a sonnet that aspires to be spirit, among poems
spirited from long restless lines, might respire a complete sentence
or clause per line, leaving as its sole exception the
line that would let its subject rest, "Content that his
lacerated memory would vanish with him." As if humanity, the
world, could be beneficent, if not forever then for once.

33.   **(Alan Dugan, "On a Myth. On a Conventional Wisdom")**

Nor, for all the attention the problem receives, can the
relation of poet to tradition be resolved into something clean
and simple. Adorno: "One must have tradition in oneself, to
hate it properly." Ad Reinhardt: "Tradition shows the artist what
not to do." Experiment grows from full absorption of, and
into, tradition, yet it simultaneously represents the antidote to tradition,
which like other antidotes (e.g. the φαρμακον in Derrida's reading
of Plato) is made of the very thing it prevents.

Line enough to allow Alan Dugan, whose absorption into tradition
echoes such moderns as Kafka and Eliot and references oracles
and the Pseudo St. Dionysus, to poke at the sonnet
(6:6:2, irregular rhymes), using it for an ironic foray into
Greek myth, watching Zeus fume over Tiresias' answer to the
question "Who has more fun in bed, men or women."

34.   (Lyrae Van Clief-Stefanon, "Eight")

George Oppen: "What one must add to the tradition is
conviction. One's own." Conviction, from the intensive of *vincere*, to
overcome. Adding another complexity to poetry's—and our own—relation
to tradition. Is it adding conviction to the tradition to
overcome tradition, or to be overcome by it? Well, both,
as appears clearly in "Eight," which depicts an attempted sexual abuse,
placed in relation to tradition by following poems about Leda
and Dinah, those exemplars of being overcome and of overcoming.

Zeus says "*I know you like me girl*," but fails
to "coax"; Dinah's brothers fight, but with pillows. Leda/Dinah speaks
for herself instead of being spoken about, and her own
conviction makes this an overcoming instead of a being overcome.
Tradition—bullets in her mother's dresser, her mother's god—needs
"other powers," and the speaker knows to call them out.

35.   (Liz Waldner, "Self Portrait As Platter On Wall")

Experiment reflects a point of view about the function and
nature of poetry, about the capacities of humans, and about
our place in the world. Its ground is metaphysical and
epistemological, not only technical. Experiment calls on poetry not to
replicate the writer's ideas or emotions in ways accessible to
the reader, but to reveal—or to create—ideas, experiences,
perspectives that do not precede it. The sonnet can succor
such a sensibility just as well as free verse can.

So even a self-portrait can seek self-discovery in preference to
self-revelation, the latter following from the former more surely than
the former from the latter. "[S]awing through my neck to
look / fixed like these" shadow puppet heads, I became "[m]y
own Salome." But here's to language. "Take my head, refreshing
foundry. / Impress, anneal. Take my head and change my mind."

36.   **(Susan Howe, "Elegiac western Imagination…")**

To view as Moses viewed after forty years of wandering
"The expanse of unconcealment / so different from all maps," so
spiritual, the rich promised land of the "Elegiac western Imagination,"
the sonnet must balance tradition with experiment, must be one
of "the spaces of drifting," one site of "Complicity battling
redemption." Must use the same word, *sere*, that "Lycidas" uses,
but as a "Mysterious confined enigma" with a fall and
swirl of its own, a falling from tree to ground.

Milton: "Truth is compared in scripture to a streaming fountain;
if her waters flow not in a perpetual progression, they
sicken into a muddy pool of conformity and tradition." Experiment
relates to tradition as flow to water: it cleanses and
purifies, allowing us therefore to find sustenance in what otherwise
would carry virulence. Blake: "Expect poison from the standing water."

37.   **(William Wordsworth, "London, 1802")**

Not that experiment as virtuous irresistible force recuperates that corrupt
immovable object, tradition. The relation is reciprocal. Experiment and tradition
alike call to tradition. "Milton! thou shouldst be living at
this hour: / England hath need of thee," having lost our
hold on our "ancient English dower" of tradition, and needing
a restoration of the elements of tradition, "manners, virtue, freedom,
power." In this case, imbalance toward experiment and away from
tradition, not vice-versa, has created "a fen / of stagnant waters."

"No wonder they insisted on those *forms!* They wouldn't know
it *was* a woman unless she was wearing a dress":
Robert Creeley means those words as critique of tradition (as
form or in another incarnation), but it can be read
also as an affirmation. Tradition offers clues to alert us
to what might be missing, or what we might miss.

38.   **(Jennifer Moxley, "Grain of the…"; "Against Aubade")**

So experimental/traditional offers a false dilemma. There is a
tradition of experiment, and one who experiments experiments with tradition.
If experimental may become traditional, "experimental" must refer to some
accidental, dynamic, fugitive characteristic, not an essential, static, permanent one.
Or refer not to the poem, but to the mind-set
of the poet. As with Pollock, who said the painter
"cannot express this age, the airplane, the atom bomb, the
radio, in the old forms of the Renaissance," then painted,
so Jennifer Moxley can call her thoughts "too awkward, too
erratic to rest / at ease in the beautiful iamb," and
then write the beautifully iambic sonnet "Against Aubade" ("Should morning's
snubbed forsaken purpose come / in love's complacent orbit to relent")
because "the mind can store old years anew," because employing
the iamb need not mean resting at ease in it.

39.   **(Miranda Field, "Wedding Night")**

Among the many objectives the attitude of experiment may pursue,
coming of age may be one. As in Miranda Field's
"Wedding Night," in which the speaker has "climbed so far
the ladder of my longing, / worked hard to glow // among
the sinking and resurrecting shadows," only to end by calling
her new husband "Pilferer, rifler, filcher," making her sonnet five
hands high on the way to that end, widely varying
the line length, employing off rhymes (bent / it, head / outside).

Experiment may offer a means of attaining or demonstrating worthiness,
as a rite of passage, leaving elders—tradition—behind to
gain autonomy or establish new affiliation. Paz: "The artist of
old wanted to be like his predecessors, to make himself
worthy of them through imitation. The modern artist wants to
be different; his homage to tradition is to deny it."

40.   **(Muriel Rukeyser, "Who in One Lifetime")**

Construing the sonnet as an act of liberation, a declaration
of independence, assumes possible, or even necessary, connection between form
and other manifestations of reality. Wittgenstein: "The possibility of its
occurring in states of affairs is the form of an
object." Which would make experiment the occasion of a new
reality. Wittgenstein again: "If we clothe ourselves in a new
form of expression, the old problems are discarded along with
the old garment." Not well-wrought urn, but document of revolution,
in which old problems, the oppressive hegemony of woman's image
as "goddess of fertility," can be engaged by, and discarded
in the face of, "childless" realities. In which "Who in
one lifetime sees all causes lost" and "knows how several
madnesses are born" may, "though her whole world burn," yet
hold "belief in the world" and be "Introspective and whole."

41.   **(John Clare, "Showers")**

In addition to ratio, turn, accumulation, and experiment, the sonnet
can be mapped onto tension and release, terms clearly related
to the others (from tension to release must be a
turn, and so on), and present to some degree in
every poem, though with clear signature in the sonnet. Even
so circumscribed a sonnet as John Clare's "Showers" depends on
tension and release, in this case manifest in the showers
that cause a human response, and in the response itself.

Clare depicts "tennants in the fields" dashing for shelter "from
the heaviest tempest." The clouds release tension as rain; the
reader experiences the laborers' tension as they "Look up and
scamper to the nearest tree." Release comes in the social
communion that gathering under one shelter provides, which biblical phrasing
identifies as spiritual communion: "Here two or three were met."

42.   (Rita Dove, "Company")

Tension in a sonnet need not be the tension of
surprise. The tension of waiting for knowledge lends mystery force,
but the tension of expectation, when knowledge arrives before event,
lends at least as much force to ancient Greek epic
and tragedy. From the beginning we know that Hektor will
die and Troy will fall, that Oedipus will discover who
murdered Laius, but tension builds in the gap between the
time of our understanding and the time of inevitable fulfillment.

When a poem in *Thomas and Beulah* opens with "No
one can help him anymore," surprise is eliminated: Thomas will
die, inevitably and soon. But in the space of expectation,
tension builds. We know what *must* happen. Foreknowledge that "There'll
be / no more trees to wake him in moonlight" intensifies
the intervening suffering: "now he can't even touch her feet."

43.   (Douglas Dunn, "The Kaleidoscope")

Even release from tension may be itself a form of
tension. Tension and release, like breathing, are cyclical: the tension
of inhalation needs exhalation as its release, and vice versa.
In "The Kaleidoscope," tension from a husband's grief over his
wife's death from cancer (one learns that from the other
elegies in the book) builds, starting with the speaker's bearing
a tray during her illness, culminating in his hands' *becoming*
a tray, "Offering me, my flesh, my soul, my skin."

The accumulated tension gets expressed as the complaint that "Grief
wrongs us so," then released: "I stand, and wait, and
cry / For the absurd forgiveness, not knowing why." I have
cried, but because "I climb these stairs a dozen times
a day," I will cry again tomorrow, and I will
need absurd forgiveness again tomorrow as I needed it today.

44.   **(Charles Bernstein, "The Kiwi Bird in the Kiwi Tree")**

Poetry's relation to reality approximates—is almost, though not quite,
as loose as—that of logic, which names one of
its aspirations validity. A valid argument manifests a necessity that
need not correlate with facts about the world. All heavenly
bodies are composed of camembert; Mars is a heavenly body;
therefore, Mars is composed of camembert. The conclusion's counterfactuality does
not diminish the argument's validity; something other than actuality may
be the stakes, in a modus ponens or a sonnet.

I may want nothing more than (other than—who says
it's more?) "the downpour of words, fecund / with tropicality," to
be a kiwi bird (flightless in actuality, quite ground-bound) in
a kiwi tree, singing to lords and ladies of Byzantium.
(My addition, but why not valid for a poem ready
to "move on / to toys or talcums, skates & scores"?)

45.   **(Jay Parini, "The Lackawanna at Dusk")**

Logic also may seek soundness, the same necessity asserted as
validity, but conjoined to imputed correlation with the actual. All
moons are made of minerals; our earth's moon is a
moon; therefore, our earth's moon is made of minerals. Whether
as argument or as sonnet, what seeks soundness says, "Here
is a river lost to nature, / running in its dead
canal / across the county, scumming its banks." It claims that
what must be must be, and that what is is.

Claims, as well, that what is affects me differently than
what must be but isn't. If for validity "Only / the
imaginary is real," and nothing else need be, for soundness
"A slow wind ushers the homely smell / around my head,"
and I see, against my will, "odds / of garbage and
poisoned fish," and "Mounds of culm burn softly into light."

46.   **(Laura Jensen, "Bad Boats")**

Canetti: "One who obeys *himself* suffocates almost as surely as
one who obeys others. Only the inconsistent one, who gives
himself orders which he then evades, does not suffocate." So
with poetic form, which may be rendered visible by rules
(fourteen lines, iambic pentameter), but application of which needs acknowledgment
of *and* resistance to rules. As wild as this world's
water is, boats are bad because they must be, and
they swagger and sway for the same reasons we do.

Shakespeare's Portia: "The brain may devise laws for the blood,
but a hot temper leaps o'er a cold decree." A
hot temper needs to rhyme "swagger" with "anchors" twelve lines
away, and "boats" with "rope" in adjacent lines; to seek
the sea's Celmins-sketched swells. Bad boats "are ready to be
bad"; "They are bad boats and they hate their anchors."

47.   (Ivor Gurney, ". . . to J.S. Bach's Memory"; "Bach—Under Torment")

What Weil says of listening to Bach could be said
of reading a sonnet: "all the faculties of the soul
become tense and silent in order to apprehend this thing
of perfect beauty, each after its own fashion. The intelligence
among the rest: it finds nothing in this thing it
hears to affirm or deny, but it feeds upon it."
The sonnet tries less to tell the truth than to
feed the hungry. The sonnet offers not correspondence but sustenance,
as Ivor Gurney implies in two sonnets to Bach, the
"Artist of four strands, eight," saying of him that "it
is predestined / That by thy chief gratitude men will make
miracles," and even praying to him as the "Father of
all makers," intercessor to "my sternest god," to "look from
your hidden / Hold where you are now and help me."

48.   (William Shakespeare, "Sonnet 19")

So, to the point, love, for which the sonnet offers
excuse, assaying and essaying both love's impossibility and its necessity.
(As logical categories, contrasted with contingency, no less than as
existential categories, one *perhaps* with an attitude, the other *probably*
with a poniard.) Love finds validation in the poem (Ortega
again: "Nothing of what we do would be our life
if we did not take account of it"), but love
also validates the poem. Neither lives long without the other.

Thus the same sonnet that pleads to time ("do whate'er
thou wilt, swift-footed Time, / To the wide world and all
her fading sweets," but "carve not with thy hours my
love's fair brow") may challenge time, because the sonnet itself
sustains love ("Yet, do thy worst, old Time. Despite thy
wrong, / My love shall in my verse ever live young").

49.   (Frank Bidart, "Love Incarnate")

Instead of giving us to understand the world better, the
sonnet offers means for enduring, and coming to treasure, the
necessity and the magnitude of our failure to understand. Instead
of relieving suffering, the sonnet asserts it as ecstasy. Bataille:
the work translates "nothing less than the moments of felicity,
the inexhaustible suffering of love." The sonnet, offered to "all
those driven berserk or humanized by love," shows love holding
in his hands "my burning heart." Love replaces, rejects, understanding.

The defining moments in a life are those in which
love changes its meaning. Such moments may be given by
entrapment in a private language, by the weather in a
godless world, by voices an owl's call evokes out of
sleep, by two green eyes of infinite depth, or by
fourteen lines that turn after eight from birth to death.

Occasions

I count myself among the "some of us" who, C. D. Wright recognizes, "do not read or write particularly for pleasure or instruction, but to be changed, healed, charged." Asked for a reading list, then, I would offer not titles per se but names of what were for me occasions.

That God might impose on me obligations I cannot justify to others or myself, I felt with *Fear and Trembling*.

That I might impose such obligations on myself, I saw in the *Twilight of the Idols*.

That my felt restlessness might mimic one of my obligations, I experienced through *Lyric Philosophy*.

That my *daimon*'s being *eu-* in another world may matter more than its being so in this one, I inferred from the *Nicomachean Ethics* and the *Crito*.

That my tracelessness does not release me from pursuing purity of motive, I inferred from *The Sovereignty of Good*.

That self-destruction might follow inevitably from passion, I took from *Anna Karenina*.

That *glukutes* could not be so *glukus* were not *pikrotes* so *pikros*, I savored when I swallowed *Eros the Bittersweet*.

That I might be one in a society of unredeemables infesting a world without redemption, I bitter-pilled from *Measure for Measure*.

That I may be pulled to death by the repulsion between my patience and my agency, I witnessed in *Gravity and Grace*.

That my very living measures my distance from the good, I understood from *Antigone*.

Changes suffered, healings desired, charges struck.

Winter Syntax

Despite its sun-faded spine and the silver star
stamped on its cover (to mark it as remaindered,
ready to be bought for a buck by a student
for whom "starving" was hyperbole and metaphor,
certainly, but not untrue), my paperback
of Herbert Morris's first book, *Peru*, gave me
a winter to mirror the one Morris parses
in a later poem on learning Latin,
or (in *this* I am his equal) failing to learn it,
though his Mrs. Goodman from junior high had
shapely calves and slender ankles to distract him
from declensions, better cause for being a boy
than I had in college, Dr. Chaney's thick
bifocals smudged from holding them by the lenses
in her arthritic fingers while the five of us
in class coughed out *hic haec hoc,* a winter that
long before I lived it Morris named, or named *at,*
in this way: *That winter was the winter syntax seemed
a route to all I thought I wished to be,* seemed the agent
through which,

> *if one could piece the sentence together,*
> *word by word, step by step, worked and reworked,*
> *if one might learn the phrasing, deep and clear,*

> *as clear as water, say, as deep as night,*
> *it might well lead, or open, to one's life;*
> *if one could learn the principle involved,*
> *one might know how to live, or what to live for.*

The principle involved in the life I still have not
learned how to live appears now as an imperative
always to refine further, to qualify
asseverations or withdraw from advances,
to progress, if progress it can be called, by
backing up, so as patron of my principle

of regress I invoke Morris, whose syntax
constantly qualifies, backs off, progresses
by regress *from darkness into darkness,* lists toward
an adequacy for which we long but which
we cannot reach, which really nothing reaches, makes
his project recognizing points of *in*adequacy,
not *his* inadequacy per se, but one
he and I share, the inevitable one,
the universal one we once called the fall.

     Morris's language, then, is Augustinian,
though importantly without promise of redemption,
a syntax that substitutes itself for naming,
that tries after the fall to do what Adam did
before, so that, though the hour be

                       too late
     to hope to gather some small strength sufficient
     to find (once more, once more, just once) the terms
     of adequate address,
                  though we sense ourselves caught
     between the wastes of self and weather,
     trying to learn ourselves, our names,
     what to make of this emptiness,
     this sense of absence which afflicts us,
we still must face the question *how shall we name*
what must be named? But if we postlapsarians
must name what *one senses transcends name or place,*
if we must fulfill Lyotard's dictum "not to
supply reality but to invent allusions
to the conceivable which cannot be presented,"
then *one should not know too soon what he waits for,*
and we can hope to accomplish nothing more than
what Morris sets his syntax to do: *hold that thought,*
defer indefinitely any closure
that might be a closing out. Even Morris's
Victorian voices and subjects get cast
as postmoderner-than-thou by his syntax,

not a syntax of the median or normal,
but a liminal syntax, out at the edge, not
on the border L=A=N=G=U=A=G=E poets map, the border
with the ungrammatical, with non-sense, but on
the one tracked by *the last train on this run, the late express,*
speeding from Disappear to Disappear, the border
with the ultra-grammatical, with hyper-sense.

    More than to any other of the goals possible
for poetry, syntax set on hypersense seeks
adequation to the Aristotelian
aspiration to conciliate one's ethics,
physics, metaphysics, and aesthetics, to make
one's words and deeds worthy of a world as little
unlike the real world as we can make it, so when
Morris speaks explicitly of the aesthetic,
of, for example, *that complication*
of discipline and passion we call art, his words
echo with the existential (the attempt *to tell you*
what I dream, what my name is, who I may be),
of the ethical (the call to care with *care, great care,*
a care so infinite one cannot weigh it),
and of the metaphysical (our givenness,
into which we fall rather than climb,

                        to deeper things,
        to darker things, to forces that, like music,
        structured the universe in affirmations
        of the intensest kind).
                    And so structured us.
    Because in all spheres our obligation exceeds
our capacity, leaving us with *damages*
here to be reported which *the mind cannot begin*
even to weigh, to estimate, to name, leaving us with,
in other words, *nothing but darkness to advance on*,
so that though we be

             not easily dissuaded
        from the effort, the hope of understanding
        what, in the end, eludes all understanding,

though our *house of words* be, like Morris's,
assembled / slowly, with great care, year by year,
our ambition nonetheless can never exceed
the ambition of Morris's syntax, can only
       keep us, for perhaps just a little longer,
       open to astonishment, to surprise,
       accessible to what one understands
       dimly, imperfectly, or not at all,
       just awhile longer, no more, just awhile.
Because what is lost when we are lost is *the long*
waiting which became our lives, Herbert Morris's
bleak, ungainly, slow syntax brings us as close
as we can hope to get to the darkness that is
falling, falling, forever falling, and that
same syntax lends me experience of the state
Morris ascribes to Joyce, the state of being
gripped by essential music, phrase by phrase.

Is Too

I'm only asking because perhaps in the end nothing is too terrible to know.

Dimensions

Jürgen Faust

As the broad problematic in his work, Jürgen Faust explores the relation between part and whole. Even his choice of "Hermeneutic Circle" as an exhibition title participates in that problematic, because the hermeneutic circle is only one manifestation—one part—of the human urge to apprehend a whole from its parts, and to divine the parts in a whole.

The part/whole problematic has a spiritual aspect, plumbed by Plato when he assigns Socrates' last argument to Simmias and Cebes, shows him persuading them that, though the body be precarious, a composition pasted from parts, the soul stands secure, an indissoluble whole; from which conclusion he further infers the ultimate project of the human spirit, to de-part the body, completing the passage to wholeness. The lover of wisdom professes dying, Socrates says, because death replaces partiality with wholeness.

Similarly, a perceptual aspect inhabits the part/whole problematic, as asserted by gestalt psychology, which attends to our minds' ability to construct from perceptual parts an intelligible whole, such that, in Michael Polanyi's words, "when focusing on a whole, we are subsidiarily aware of its parts, while there is no difference in the intensity of the two kinds of awareness." As happens when we look at a face: we are as aware of the eyes as of the whole face, though the awareness of the face is primary, and of the eyes subsidiary. A part subsidiary to a whole must help sustain our perception of the whole, and that sustenance we call *meaning*.

By conceptualizing his work in terms of the hermeneutic circle, Faust foregrounds the temporal aspect of the part/whole problematic. As explicated in *Being and Time*, the hermeneutic circle is that process of understanding, which, according to Heidegger, corresponds to the structure of meaning, and ultimately to Being itself. It is not a vicious circle, but one to be willingly sought and undertaken. "What is decisive is not to get out of the circle, but to get in it in the right way. This circle of understanding is not a circle in which any random kind of knowledge operates, but it is rather the expression of the existential *fore-structure* of Da-sein itself."

Whatever its metaphysical validity or ontological basis, the hermeneutic circle is, as a process, temporal, a sequence of actions aimed at grasping a whole. A person confronted with an image always performs, Gadamer claims, "an act of projecting. He projects before himself a meaning" for the whole image, which the parts, by their divergence from that projection, lead him to revise. "The working out of this fore-project, which is constantly revised in terms of what emerges," is how one synthesizes an understanding of a whole. Faust's work brings to conscious awareness this typically autonomic activity.

To ask the question of part and whole, though, and to draw out awareness of our hermeneutic activities, Faust applies as his method the presentation of a part *as* a whole. Because the divergence of phenomena from what we project leads us to revise our understanding, Faust exaggerates that divergence, giving us neither accustomed subjects nor accustomed modes of representation. As with the part/whole problematic itself, so with the method of presenting a part as the whole are there manifestations in various fields. In science, chaos theory observes the replication of parts as wholes; in mathematics, fractals flower from parts counted as wholes; theologies depend on accepting microcosm for macrocosm; literature makes use of a type of metaphor called synecdoche, in which a part stands for the whole; and human civil society can occur only on the basis of some form of representation, a way of deploying a part as the whole.

Faust's aim, formulated in aesthetic terms, is to trouble the relationship between the wholeness of the work and the wholeness of its subject. At least in the history of European painting, if not also in other periods and locales and media of art, the objective has been most often to attempt to make the whole subject fill, but fit within, the whole canvas. (This explains why the cutting down of a Rembrandt seems such a travesty: vast presumption on the part of whoever authorized it, for believing he or she knew better than the painter knew what the whole subject of the painting is. And why we regard composition—the arrangement of parts with respect to the whole—as so high up the hierarchy of aesthetic values.) Some critics, e.g. Derrida with his explorations of the parergon and the frame, have questioned in theory the truthfulness of (purported) identity between whole work and whole subject; Faust questions it in his practice.

In addition to interrogating the work, Faust interrogates the medium. The parts he presents as wholes remind the viewer that the medium is not ourselves, that it reveals wholes we might not otherwise see, or creates wholes we might not otherwise create, and thus reveals the arbitrariness (Faust uses the words "subjectivity" and "playfulness") of any whole. Faust's works also remind the viewer that the medium is not its subject. Any whole a given medium represents is only a part of what it seeks to represent: Faust's video of a marketplace, 24 hours compressed to 2.4 minutes, is not the marketplace itself. A third reminder about medium is the interdependency of medium and whole. If anything can serve as a medium (a stone floor may register a drawing), then any whole gets determined in part by what the particular medium can host. The stone floor can host only a spatial whole such as a drawing or sculpture, not a temporal whole such as a video.

Emphasizing its aesthetic aspects makes Faust's project sound effete, conceptually rich but at one remove from reality, but the dilemma Faust presents (in his words, that "it isn't possible to understand any one part of a work until you understand the whole, but it also isn't possible to understand the whole without also understanding all of the parts") has an existential aspect as well. As Plato repeatedly points out in dialogues about living a good life, in order to decide whether a given action is good, one would need to know what the Good is. And the dilemma applies to any end sought—virtue, self-interest, profit, pleasure. One would need to know the whole, in other words, to ascertain whether an item is a part of the whole. By distributing the dilemma across time, as Faust does in this work (nowhere more clearly than in "the hour we didn't know anything from each other"), the hermeneutic circle offers a way out of the dilemma: fore-understanding and revision constitute a process for resolving the dilemma. Aesthetic work and existential work alike become hypothesis, a putting forward, which helps explain the anti-romantic flavor of the work: it stands in opposition to the Kantian preference for the categorical over the hypothetical.

That anti-romantic quality might also be construed as an ascetic quality, but no such ascesis attends this work. The sensual can be naïve and polymorphously perverse, an enjoyment of perception analogous to Freudian infantile sexuality. The aesthetic imposes cultural influence on, and direction of, the senses, gives the senses rules to follow, as according to Freud the moral imposes cultural influence on the sexual. Faust's work asserts, and appeals to, a post-aesthetic sensuality, a sensuality "after experience." This body of work presents, and invites the viewer into, a sensuality not numbed or negated by a reflective aesthetic, but enlivened by it.

Suzanne Chamlin

Suzanne Chamlin does not draw hills and trees, recording perceptions on paper to pose her viewers opposite the subject as bystanders. Instead, her "perceptual and more interior connections to nature" link her viewers meditatively to the hills and trees. Unlike the nineteenth-century American landscape painters who portrayed landscape as a threat, the Kantian sublime bullying us into awe of its majesty, Chamlin portrays the landscape as an entreaty, Platonic beauty seducing us to contemplation of its integrity. She does not *draw* landscapes, she *draws on* them. A mystic, she imposes no barrier between real and imaginary, outer world and inner.

Arguing that "pure drawing is an abstraction," Cézanne abstracted shapes to suggest natural forms, showing us trees and apples as differentiations of color, pushing the viewer back through color patches on canvas to the natural forms they represent. Picasso used abstraction as synthetic form, converting the canvas into a kaleidoscope on which fragments tumble, depicting principles of arrangement in preference to things arranged. Suzanne Chamlin, playing Picasso against Cézanne, uses natural forms to suggest abstractions. If Cézanne's abstract shapes suggest the trees of Mont Sainte-Victoire, Chamlin's trees of Virginia and hillsides of Spain suggest the abstractions of Rothko or Frankenthaler.

Suzanne Chamlin's paintings embody oppositions, including observation vs. memory, perception vs. imagination, outside vs. inside, nature vs. the studio, momentary vs. permanent. By continually transforming each pole into the other, Chamlin's works assume a robust version of the double identity in the duckrabbit or Necker cube. Each work transforms observation into memory, memory into observation, and so on. "I have always been interested in the experience of starting with one thing and making it into another." Through that process, each work replays on its own stage and in its own scale the Rilkean dictum that "you must revise your life."

Transformations like the movement between perception and imagination enrich Chamlin's work and its viewers. "Exploring the tension between real and imaginary landscape," both painter and painted inhabit the landscape, enabling it to serve the viewer as what Eugenijus Ališanka calls "the landscape of the soul." Chamlin thus fulfills her ambition "to describe a sense of place, time, a moment," not by preserving the moment like an insect fixed in amber or a fetus in formaldehyde, but by recreating in oils or ink the Augustinian present moment, inhabited by past and future, by temporal humanity and eternal deity.

"I work with light," Suzanne Chamlin says, "as I experience it directly, as well as in memory and imagination." But light does not willingly suffer being "worked with." As shape must be reduced in a painting or drawing from three dimensions to two, presenting depth as an illusion created by height and breadth, so light must be reduced from three dimensions to two, presenting brightness as an illusion created by hue and saturation. In Chamlin's works, light retains its fullness in all moods: intense light searing Spanish scrub to complex light through coastal clouds or hazy light hugging Virginia hills.

Suzanne Chamlin's works sustain both "contradictory impulses" that William

Gass says fight in any art: "the impulse to communicate and so to treat the medium of communication as a means, and the impulse to make an artifact out of the materials of the medium and so to treat the medium as an end." Dominance by either compromises a work. Made only as a means, a work becomes tendentious and didactic; made only as an end, a work becomes effete. The quality of Chamlin's paintings and drawings shows in their unwillingness to decide between the two impulses, to surrender their balance.

Ursula von Rydingsvard

The 1996 Hudson Hills Press book on Ursula von Rydingsvard opens with an essay by Dore Ashton, which itself opens with this anecdote: "I once asked Ursula von Rydingsvard if she could remember her earliest artistic experience. After a thoughtful pause, she answered: 'I remember something about unbleached, coarse linen. It would almost take its own form. I remember its being on me, almost like a nightgown—something about light on my body. Maybe I was three or four … outdoors, on the steps.'" Ashton expresses surprise at von Rydingsvard's answer. "I had expected her to remember some picture she had seen as a child, or perhaps her first drawing. But what she remembered was, in effect, a sculpture."

Ashton's surprise at von Rydingsvard's answer reflects a pervasive cultural error that manifests itself as Ashton's assumption, which all of us pre-reflectively share, that drawing is the primitive and primary form of art. Ontogenetically, we likely picture children's art as stick figures holding three-fingered hands next to a house with a curlicue of smoke crayoned above the chimney. Phylogenetically, we think of hunters and hunted on the caves of Lascaux. Like Ashton, we all would have been surprised by von Rydingsvard's answer. Ashton is alert, though: she catches herself in the mistake, and corrects for it. I hope to do the same here, using von Rydingsvard, just as Ashton does, as my prompt.

Von Rydingsvard's inversion, her presenting a sculptural experience rather than an experience of drawing as primitive, establishes an opposition between drawing and sculpture that I take to reflect a deeper opposition, that between observation and immersion. The opposition may be suggested by the following chart.

	1. Ashton/us/Western culture	2. von Rydingsvard
art form	drawing	sculpture
mode of inquiry	mimetic	sensory
process of inquiry	depiction	materialization
stance of inquirer	observation (spectator)	immersion (participant)
means of inquiry	metaphor (likeness)	immediacy (presence)
object of inquiry	what the world is like	that I am in the world

We are surprised by von Rydingsvard's answer because we have followed philosophers in taking column 1 as primary. We have done so in a way, and to a degree, that corrupts self-understanding and understanding of the world. Column 1 does appear to be uniquely human. We seem to be the only species that (without prompting by zealous zookeepers) draws pictures, the only species that uses metaphor, the only species whose members construe themselves as spectators of their own lives. But even if (1) is uniquely human, it does not follow that it is autonomous and complete in itself. (2) *must* be autonomous and complete in itself: if non-human animals do not "do" column 1, then they must be doing column 2 and only column 2. One might be immersed without also being a spectator, as we typically think, say, prairie dogs are. They don't observe themselves as prairie dogs, we say, or reflect on the significance of life on the high plains, or draw self-portraits. They just do prairie-dog things: burrow, scamper, frolic. But from other animals' doing *only* column 2, and humans' doing column 1, it does not follow that humans do *only* column 1. Pretending that we do only column 1, or that we *ought* to do only column 1, or even that we *could*, results in further absurdities: skepticism, solipsism, so-called "postmodernism."

At least since Plato, art has been assumed to be in its essence mimetic. Aristotle solidified the view I am here questioning, that art is mimetic because *we ourselves* are mimetic. We are, Aristotle argues, the creatures who copy. Rational animals, yes, but even more essentially, mimetic animals. In the history of philosophy, sensation has been consistently treated as at best a means toward the (higher) end of mimesis, or at worst a diversion from that higher end. Yet mimesis is the source of art's unreliability and danger: it does not give us, Plato reminds us, the reality of what it imitates, but a copy, a postiche, a fake.

I affirm the existence and the value of the whole of column 1, and of each item in it. I am happy to extend to all of art what, in *Poetry at One Remove*, John Koethe says very elegantly of poetry: "Something poetry, in the broadest sense, aspires to is an understanding of what it is *like* to be whatever it is we are. This is something we need in order to even begin to understand *what* it is we are. Whatever a self or subject is, each of us certainly 'is' one, and our experiences are the experiences 'of' one. So poetry ought to be able to help us understand what our kind of subject is." Art ought to help us understand in this way: understand what *kind* of subject we are, understand what it is like to be as we are. That is, art ought to do column 1 things, and it does do them. I only mean to assert that column 1 is not, and cannot be, fully realized without column 2. Any time we try to operate fully in column 1 (in art or in philosophy or in any other practice), we run aground: we arrive at some form of despair and alienation, be it skepticism or solipsism or entrapment in the medium of the practice.

The inferences behind the mistake—the reasons for making it—seem obvious once the columns are laid out in this way. The columns can be *distinguished* from one another, and column 2 can be (and most often is) realized in *separation* from column 1, so we assume the relation must be symmetrical: column 1 must also be susceptible to separation from column 2. From this it is easy to take the next step, and infer that, if column 1 is the exclusively human column, and if the two are separable, it must be best for humans to realize column 1 *exclusively*, to live *only* in column 1. But not so. The columns may be *distinguished* from one another, and column 2 may be *separated* from column 1, but column 1 may *not* be *separated* from column 2. Prairie dogs can live immersed as participants in their lives without also observing themselves as spectators of their lives, but we humans cannot observe our lives without also being immersed in them. Prairie dogs can sense without copying, but we cannot copy without sensing. Prairie dogs can be immediately aware (sensing a coyote nearby, say) but not metaphorically aware (of the coyote's eyes glowing like stars in a cloudless sky). And so on. Consequently, even if we adopt, as well we might, the ideal that realization of column 1 as fully and robustly as possible is good for humans, we must forfeit the ideal that realization of column 1 *exclusively* would be good for us.

But that latter ideal, the mistaken one, is exactly the ideal Western philosophies and religions have most often adopted, by distinguishing soul from body, placing soul exclusively in column 1 and body exclusively in column 2, and asserting the superiority of soul over body. There it is in Plato, when Socrates asserts in the *Apology* that philosophers make dying their profession, i.e. that one seeks to liberate the soul entirely from the body, and again in the *Republic* in the allegory of the cave and the divided line, and so on. There it is also in St. Paul, who starts his letter to the Romans by distinguishing spiritual circumcision from (mere) physical circumcision, starts his first letter to the Corinthians by distinguishing spiritual people from people of the flesh, and so on.

To return, now, to Ursula von Rydingsvard's work. The distribution of terms into the two columns of the chart suggests that more is at stake in von Rydingsvard's sculpture than appears on casual viewing. Her work contests a pervasive but inadequate understanding of art and ourselves and the world, and invites a re-vision. It realizes column 2:

- Obviously its chosen art form or medium is sculpture, rather than drawing.
- It is not copying anything, real or ideal. The work asks us to touch it, perhaps, but not to *pass through* it to what it copies, as we may be invited to pass through a Bierstadt to the sublime landscape it represents.
- Von Rydingsvard's work is not primarily about the image one sees in the piece, but about the material presence of the piece, not its ideal re-presentation of something other than itself, but its real im-position of itself.
- It is not primarily asking us to observe it in a detached, "objective" way, but to immerse ourselves in it, be "absorbed" by it, treating not its surface but its materiality as fundamental.
- It is not essentially comparative. It does not present itself as *like* something else (as a portrait is like the sitter, or an icon is like the Blessed Virgin), but asserts its own nonmetaphorical immediacy.
- It does not attempt primarily to tell me something about the world I hadn't known before, but to remind me I am here.

Our category "art" may mislead us in various ways, starting with its elision of drawing and sculpture. The assumption that sculpture and drawing both belong to art as subcategories asks us to treat them similarly; the assumption that drawing is primary asks us to treat sculpture as drawing with one more dimension. I have tried to contest such treatment, by regarding drawing as no more primary than sculpture, and the two as profoundly different from one another. I have tried to give reason to believe that because of their difference from one another, drawing and sculpture imply different postures toward the work, ourselves, and the world, and to suggest that the posture implied by sculpture is essential to humanity, not a base posture to be transcended by humanity.

Garry Noland

The work in Garry Noland's "Unorganized Territory" wrestles first of all with genre: the pieces would be best described as collages, but they veer toward painting; and they are pragmatically two-dimensional (they fit in frames and hang on walls), but spiritually three-dimensional (made on board that rises from the mat, or built up topographically). All are landscapes, but with various divergences from the usual approach.

The works group themselves, most noticeably by size, into four ranges: four works, each roughly 70"x50"; three roughly 30"x45" each; ten in varying dimensions in the range of 12"x10"; and a multitude of palm-sized pieces, roughly 5"x4" each. The size groupings are not arbitrary; they reflect subtle variations on the themes the works share in common. The largest pieces, the loosest and the most abstract, con-sist of tellurian shapes constructed from paper colored with oil paint or watercolor, resembling mountain ranges seen from above. The next largest group also builds its paper hills up from the surface and colors them with watercolor, but from a different perspective: instead of occupying a position directly overhead, the viewer has moved down low enough for a horizon to enter the work. The viewer continues her descent in the two smaller sets of works, and the descent becomes metaphorical as well, since several express in their titles indebtedness to Dante.

Noland's show explores reciprocities between land and food. The background for the first of the largest works, for instance, is made from pages of an old text on the chemistry of food; it contains such headings as "hydrolysis of proteins" and "fat solvents." Throughout the show, pictures of meat cut, one supposes, from magazines and cookbooks, get transformed by collage into geological formations, thus drama-tizing in the work the problematic relationship between human food consumption and the land. Animal welfare, sustainable agriculture, and related issues all inhabit the works as visual presences.

Although mounted in a position that makes it the last work a visitor sees, the oldest piece in the show, "Scenes from Roald Amundsen's Polar Expedition," serves to introduce the rest. Consisting of twenty-five of the smallest-size collages, individually framed and hung in a row at eye level, plus a map of Amundsen's expedition, the piece takes the viewer on a journey that is ambiguously historical and fantastic, indicating Noland's eerie overlay of imagined landscapes over real ones. To my mind the pieces with the most distinctive vision are the 12"x10" group. Each is made on an irregularly shaped (roughly rectangular) piece of wood. Somewhere on the wood, seeming to pierce through the background rather than to rest on top of it, sits a circle bordered by numbers designating compass points, and containing a landscape. "Real" items like cuts of meat become "abstract" as they compose the landscape, and the viewer is placed by the circular border (like a scope or a porthole) in a claustrophobic space that looks out onto an immeasurable space.

For all of Noland's obsessiveness, thanks to which his work maintains a thematic and stylistic continuity, his restlessness asserts itself and makes the work continue to explore new ground, as the name of this show suggests. "Territory" comes from the Latin "terra," meaning earth or land. But "organized" comes from the Latin "organum," itself derived from the Greek "organon," which means (a) an instrument, implement, or tool, (b) the material of a work, or (c) the work, the product itself. Indeed, the English word "work," though it may not look much like "organized," comes from the same root, since "organon" derives from "ergon," which with its original digamma would have been pronounced "wergon." Strangely, the English word "organic" comes from "organon" as well, rather than from the Greek "orgao," which means to swell with moisture, or (of soil) to teem with produce, or (of animals) to lust. So when Noland declares his territory *un*organized, he asserts its *non*instrumentality. He adapts the Kantian "always as an end and never simply as a means" to nature, as Jan Zwicky does when in a passage on ecology she defines exploitation as using a thing "in the absence of a perception of what it *is*." The paradox at the axis of Garry Noland's work is that these "imaginary," "fantastic" landscapes show us truths about the "real" earth that "realistic" depictions could not show.

Noland's work confronts us with the inevitability of our interaction with the earth: we shape it, but it also shapes—and has shaped—us. The result is an image like "The Americas," which can be construed as a map (a visible assertion of our shaping the earth) or as a smoldering volcano (the earth's shaping force made visible). We learn who we are by observing what we are not. If I were identifying a predecessor for this work, then, it would be not an artist but the British geologist Charles Lyell, who showed, over one hundred and fifty years ago, some of the implications an understanding of geologic time has for human self-understanding: Darwin's *Origin of Species* became possible only after Lyell's *Principles of Geology* gave natural selection millions of years, instead of a few thousand, in which to work. Knowing how old the earth is, and the pace and scale of its developments and alterations, tells us a great deal about ourselves. Garry Noland's "Unorganized Territory" follows Lyell's lead, imaging geology as a way of imagining ourselves.

Jim Sajovic

God grants us access to paradise on the basis of vision, not virtue. Precise and replete perception, not asceticism or obedience, conjures paradise. To such a heresy does Jim Sajovic subscribe in this sybaritic body of work, and such would be its sermon did it preach.

But no homilies harangue us here, in this garden that grows out of Bosch, not the Bible. Sajovic's *Millennium* triptych speaks as Bosch's speaks, in symbols "not born of a dualistic dialogue between idea and form but of perfectly simultaneous acts of seeing and thinking."

Adam and Eve fell when the serpent persuaded them of something super-sensible, beyond their bodies, that demanded obedience but withheld delight. They fell not into flames, but into bottomless darkness, anesthesia, each weightless body tumbling out of reach of the other.

Fraenger infers that Bosch's *Garden of Earthly Delights* could not have called Catholics, but must have spoken to a sect, the *Homines Intelligentiae*, radical Ad-amites who believed "the ancient breach between spirit and libido can be bridged— in defiance of death and the devil."

Sajovic's *Millennium Garden*, too, speaks to *homines* who *percipiunt* through *intelligentis*, rather than to those who *cognoscunt* through *ratio*. Instead of the spirits who directed Odysseus and Dante to hell and back, Sajovic, like Bosch, adopts bodies as guides to all three worlds.

Thus Sajovic celebrates sexuality as a divine effulgence, unlike Schiele, say, who sees only its consuming beauty. Sajovic's triptych pushes the devouring maw to one side, unlike Schiele's "Reclining Nude Girl," where, as in Lear's madness, the sulphurous pit slits the center.

But how show the body so, in its sinless shine? Process, material, rapture. Sajovic switched sketchbook for screen, composing these paintings with Photoshop and toner in place of pen and ink. A scanner lent them luxury (abundance and license, from the Latin for light).

Sajovic animated them with mica chips mixed in the paint. Move right to left, back and forth. The figures switch from green to blue, the ground from gold to red. The bodies advance and recede. They flicker and fall as if they had souls, or indeed as if they were souls.

The devout, Solomon to Plato to Bosch to Donne to Bernini to Berryman, have recognized the religiosexual double entendre in *rapture*: carried off as prey, raped, transported to mental ecstasy, borne to heaven. So the bodies in these soulscapes beckon: *This is my body. Take. Eat.*

Warren Rosser

Four principal problems preoccupy painters: depth, meaning, light, and motion.

To achieve depth, a painter must fit three dimensions onto a two-dimensional surface. To create meaning, he or she must imbue physical materials with semiological character. To portray light, the painter must, from the two properties of color manipulable in pigments, hue and saturation, conjure a third, brightness, which, though not variable in paint, is in nature light's most immediate manifestation to human perception. To represent motion, the artist must defy the static nature of the medium.

Viewing Warren Rosser's work in relation to these four problems helps to site it, in two ways. First, historically, it indicates why Rosser's work matters so much, and why it matters *now*. The four problems might be seen as a cycle, each supplanting the one preceding it to create a new artistic epoch. The Egyptians and Greeks explored depth, chasing dimensionality from stick figure to solidity. To Medieval Europe meaning mattered most, so they savored icons, surfaces suffused with semiosis. The metamorphosis of meaning into light, begun in the Renaissance, sustained the Italians, the Dutch, and the French for centuries, prompting painters as otherwise various as Michelangelo, Vermeer, and Monet. The twentieth century, starting early with Cézanne's shimmering landscapes and continuing through more blatant abstractions, including nudes descending staircases and action paintings, sought motion in a fixed medium.

One century cannot become another without passing through some seminal work that contains both. Like *Lyrical Ballads* in 1800, and *The Interpretation of Dreams* in 1900, "Hybrid View" could serve that purpose for our centuries, since, however else they speak, and whatever else they do, Warren Rosser's recent works *move*. That they are so insistently animate places these paintings and prints as fulfillments of painting's historical progression, and if one thinks of the prey depicted on the walls of Lascaux as solutions to the problem of depicting motion, and thus of the progression as a cycle, Rosser stands at the beginning as well.

Viewed according to this historical progression, Rosser's own ontogeny reca-pitulates painting's phylogeny. The recent history of Rosser's work shows him em-phasizing the various problems in turn: dimensionality in his wooden constructions of the late 1980s and early 1990s (Rosser's kouros and kore figures); iconography in his 1995 "Dislocated Emblems" show (his altarpieces); the emphasis on color in late-1990s work (his landscapes and maps, which soon grow mazes and tracks); and motion in his "Hybrid View." Such restlessness in an artist, such stubborn refusal merely to replicate previous successes, is itself a movement, and had to draw out motion in the work.

The four problems also help site Rosser's work methodologically. The historical progression of the problems implies that any painting will emphasize the solution to one problem over the others, but emphasis on one problem does not relieve it from the need to solve the others. Every painting must solve all four. Rosser's paintings and prints emphasize motion, but they solve each problem in a compelling way. They solve the problem of depth through layering, as a print like "Circuit Overlap"—even through its title—indicates. The yellow-green shape on the lower right is partially above and partially below the underpainting. The outlined shapes, which the eye wants to place behind the solid shapes, press to the front. The squeegeed rectangles at the lower left veil the black shape. And the varied colors of the underpainting, with their suggestion of blurred reflections on water and of watery scenes on Chi-nese scrolls, recede. Even the impressions in the paper contribute to the sense of depth.

Rosser solves the problem of meaning through overdetermination. Though hardly dreamy, with their "wired" colors and emphatic shapes, these paintings do share one of the characteristics that make dreams fascinating, namely overdetermi-nation. What appears in these paintings, like what appears in dreams, can sustain multiple, and even contradictory, meanings. Consider the recurring shape, an oval with an extended rectilinear form emerging from it, perpendicular to the oval's long axis. This shape might be construed as a hammer, a sperm cell, a stingray, a mush-room, a mushroom cloud, a piston, an electron, a human figure, a tree, a comet, or any of a hundred other possibilities from the natural, the human, and the technological realms. And the contexts in which the shapes recur sustain the multiplicity of pos-sible interpretations.

The works in "Hybrid View" solve the problem of light through contrast. In Albersian fashion, the color of a given shape establishes itself by its relation to the other colors in the piece. This becomes especially clear in the grouped prints and the segmented paintings, where the same pigment used in two mushrooms presents an entirely different color against one background than against another.

These paintings and prints solve their central problem, the problem of motion, in two divergent, almost contradictory, ways: phoronomically and by blending. The orientation of the shapes relative to the canvas or paper and in relation to one another determines the direction and speed of their motion. When they are oriented with the stem parallel to the shorter dimension of the canvas, they seem to move sideways, and when they are oriented with the stem parallel to the longer dimension, they seem to move ahead. When they are oriented in line with one another, they seem to move in a line, and when they are oriented around an axis, they appear to turn. The degree to which they blend with the underpainting and the degree to which the underpainting itself is blurred determine the speed at which they appear to move.

These works, made without using a brush, continue Rosser's ongoing technical investigations, which over the past fifteen years have included unpainted three-dimensional wooden constructions, painted wooden constructions, drawings of the shadows of constructions, mixed media constructions emerging from but connected to the wall, and so on. However, it is as conceptual investigations that these works have their greatest power. Their movements confront us with abstraction as drawing out (its etymological sense, from the same root that gives "traction" and "tractor"); their dimensions insist on a relation to the human body ("Primary Slippage" is 24" tall, the height of a toddler learning to walk, and 72" wide, the length of an adult lying down to die; "Pin Wheel—Arrested Movement," at 137", is just as wide as two humans are tall); their overdetermination undermines our fixing on a sense of scale (are these galaxies or subatomic particles?); their Bach-like attention to the potential implicit in pattern makes them almost musical. Thus Warren Rosser's works fulfill in a paradigmatic way two basic functions of art, inducement to pleasure and provocation to thought.

Lester Goldman

All this standing stiffly puzzling over paintings hung in high-ceilinged rooms, looking contemplative, whispering to avoid a scowl from the guard, reciting Rilke—"Almost everything serious is difficult, and everything is serious"—has gone on entirely too long. How about a note of Nietzsche here? "I would believe only in a god who could dance. And when I saw my devil I found him serious, thorough, profound, and solemn: it was the spirit of gravity—through him all things fall. Not by wrath does one kill but by laughter. Come, let us kill the spirit of gravity."

Let us beat the spirit of gravity, Lester Goldman grins, like a rag doll. A rag ball rag doll. Let him take his lumps. We'll have a ball. Like it or lump it. Who'll oil her manic one each morning? I volunteer. My erotic fantasy always disguises itself as religious ecstasy, and my religious ecstasy as erotic fantasy. It's gotten so I can't tell them apart, but at this rag ball it seems not to matter.

And this rag *is* a ball. A little Scott Joplin for the canvas. Syncopation. Syncopaintin'. The first word is *welcome*. The figure never disappears. The ragged masses dance on through the ragged night. Raggedly. Doggedly whirling. Dizzily wearing their inner ears on their sleeves.

China Marks

"I suspect myself to be half P. T. Barnum and half Jane Goodall." No ordinary self-description that, spoken by no ordinary artist.

P. T. Barnum might disclaim paternity, but his showmanship still flows in China Marks's arteries. No element more pervades her work than drama. Seldom do her works depict a solitary object; more often they show two, three, or more characters in open conflict or in compromising situations. "Untitled (#7)" exemplifies the imbroglios into which the relationships often knot themselves: one figure thinks of another who reflects on a cross, while holding on her lap a third figure, who watches a costume/puppet animated by a fourth figure, from whose mouth a head emerges. No one figure focuses attention; the viewer's eye must wander from figure to figure in an attempt to incorporate all. A different drama animates "Riders to an Inland Sea," which foregrounds four figures, two riding, two being ridden: as in many of China Marks's works, the interrelationships between the depicted subjects do not exhaust the interrelationships engendered by the drawing. One ridden figure looks down to hell, the other up to heaven, but both riders look out from the picture plane, invoking and rendering complicit the viewer.

Even when only one character appears, it manifests the schizophrenic split inherent in humans, the split Plato called the tripartite soul, Freud designated as id/ego/superego, and Theodore Roethke celebrated in song: "We are one, and yet we are more, / I am told by those who know,—/ At times content to be two." In "Portrait of the Artist as a Moral Idiot," for example, the central figure grasps and ingests—or expectorates—a shadow self, and in "Untitled (#9)," the unity or separation between the two figures remains ambiguous: do they make one person or two?

The drama of multiplicity appears in other ways as well. Marks's protagonists mimic Proteus, by perpetually mutating, morphing from one creature into another. These works show us dog-boys and bird-girls, devil-people and dinosaur-people. No identity remains fixed, although (true to Einstein's law) what China Marks's world sacrifices in stability it makes up for in energy.

If her Barnumesque dramaturgy barks to all bystanders, Marks's consanguinity with Jane Goodall announces itself more subtly, in her commitment to the accuracy of observation that Wallace Stevens calls "the equivalent of accuracy of thinking." The subtlety lies in distortion. Poets and novelists try to tell the truth, but they do so precisely by lying; visual artists try to depict one reality by creating another. China Marks creates not a Borgesian map that *is* the territory, but a map that maps our world by being a world parallel to our own. She sees our world by seeing something else, as have all mystics and visionaries. All the efforts of the Hebrew Patriarchs and Euro American Protestants to construct an aniconic god fall away beside the sixteen-square-foot asseveration of idolatry China Marks calls "Bird Girl Gets 'Sanctified.'" Moses may have seen no more than God's backside, but Bird Girl looks into His eyes. Martin Luther may not have seen God, but China Marks has.

Its genealogical accuracy aside, Marks's Barnum/Goodall self-description also names her androgynous artistic nature. Not epicene—void of sexual characteristics—but sexually overdetermined, celebrating *all* sexual possibility, polymorphously perverse. China Marks sings with Walt Whitman, "I will show of male and female that either is but the equal of the other. / And sexual organs and acts! do you concentrate in me, for I am determin'd to tell you with courageous clear voice to prove you illustrious." Some of the works wear their sexuality on their sleeves, as in the finger-fucking in "Untitled (# 12)," but at least as many make their sexuality more ambiguous or implicit. Is there a hint of anal intercourse in "Riders to an Inland Sea" or more than a hint? Is the bondage there sexual? As in Freud, so in these paintings and drawings: every part of the body becomes an erotogenic zone, and every object a sexual object.

China Marks describes the "parallel world" depicted in her work as "primarily an oral society." Oral, I would add, in more ways than one, and in no way more obvious than in the mouths of its denizens. Many mouths, disproportionately large mouths, voracious mouths. China Marks's work portrays a labial parallel world, from earlier sculptures like "Loss" and "The Player and the Played" through these recent paintings like "Prisoner of Childhood." "Those Whom the Gods Love," she tells us in title and drawing alike, "They Eat Slowly." In the sculptures with which China Marks began and matured her artistic vision, in such pieces as "Domestic Drama" and "Trio with Spoon," the characters eat each other politely, with utensils, but in her current work, the characters, now ravenous, eat each other whole.

In addition to the orality of mouths and tableware, the orality of words marks these works. Any land speaks a language, and China Marks portrays a polyglot parallel world, but her titles reveal at least one of the languages as our own. Many of her titles use jokes, puns, allusions, or double entendres. In "Baby Buggy," for example, the word "buggy" means infested with bugs (as the painting so obviously is), bug-like (as the baby becomes when its two legs are added to the high-chair's four), and crazy (as who wouldn't be in such a household), besides calling to mind the tongue-twister "rubber baby buggy bumpers." Similarly, the title "Flesh Wounds" (like the drawing it names) might be read with "flesh" as an adjective modifying the noun "wounds," or with "flesh" as the noun and "wounds" as a verb.

In addition to their titular cerberations, words occasionally bubble to the surface in the drawings, as in "Hope and Despair Greet the New Century," where enigmatic phrases ("Awkward as a young girl at her first dance . . .") mix with aperçus ("Of course, to despair is to deny our children their future . . ."). More persistently, though, these works speak a *visual* language, in which the recurring elements, from animal parts to bones to ropes and chains to enclosures, create a code that makes Marks's corpus the score of the humming you will hear in your head when you close your eyes tonight.

In addition to the artist's self-description, one might find other flints to strike against these works, for they are hard and give off sparks. Look to *Lear*. In that bleak world, that *nihilo* from which we are not *ex*ed, the character who sees most clearly is the fool. As in Lear's world, so in ours, where death no less inevitably ends all: "if the fool" (Blake says) "would persist in his folly he would become wise." In *Lear*, that most tragic tragedy, wisdom nests in the comic. So too in China Marks's works. No less portentous than *Lear*, these paintings and drawings are no less frequently *funny*. Look at the serviced woman's expression in "Room Service," or imagine how a child might react to "Untitled (# 7)." Fools can disarm us long enough to raise questions we might not ask otherwise. What *does* a fool in striped pants know of the devil? *Is* there a circus on Mars?

If Greek sculpture perfected the representation of three dimensions in three dimensions, and Renaissance perspective perfected the representation of three dimensions in two dimensions, then twentieth-century visual artists (like their contemporaries in physics and psychology and poetry) work under the obligation to represent more dimensions than three. Physicists now speak of twenty dimensions and more, and artists too must synthesize/synesthetize more dimensions than length, breadth, and depth. China Marks aspires to such a synthesis. Her mixtures of media lend complexity to individual works and the oeuvre; her imbrications of pattern and figure and the consequent interpenetrations of perspective and flatness force the eye to find its own way through each piece; her titles infuse another medium, spoken language, into the work; her teratological figures invoke mythology and dreams. These works speak to our sexual selves, our religious selves, our contemplative selves, and our primitive reptilian selves. Their rich entanglements culminate in "A Grown Woman," the most recent piece in the show, by becoming the liana depicted there. Profuse and lush, they grow around us and take our own shapes, becoming a polydimensional cast that will stand after our passing.

These works compress whole histories into themselves: simultaneously etiological and eschatological, they embody the identity of end and beginning T. S. Eliot nods to in *Four Quartets*. Not only in the ubiquitous sexual birth/deaths of their subjects and in the messages each medium channels into the whole do these works show us our end in our beginning, but also qua art, which can become its own future only by re-presenting its past. Knowledge grants gravidity, and China Marks knows all the art she can bear. Sometimes her re-presentation announces itself, as in "The Temptation of St. Anthony" and the fools that recall Picasso's harlequins, but more often it works tacitly, as in "Room Service," where the entangled lovers and their homunculus cannot but call to mind Leonardo's "Virgin and St. Anne," their legs emerging from beneath their drapes, the impish boy nearby.

China Marks's uroboric works, then, insist that this meditation end as it began, with the artist's own words: these drawings and paintings create for their viewer "a stroll, a scramble, a trek, a climb through a vast *terra incognita* full of wonderful plants and animals and ravishing vistas at every turn."

A Conversation with Philip Metres

Philip Metres: *Thanks for getting together to talk about your work, which I found fascinating on a number of levels. It seems like there are, right now, a lot of poetic responses to the Iraq War, and even more if you draw back to post-9/11. One of the things that struck me about* God Bless *in relation to your past work is the intense formal operation that underlies the book, its obsessive proceduralism. And yet, your work to date has not been explicitly political in the way that this book is. I wondered if you would talk about what sorts of procedural rules you set for yourself to write these poems, particularly in relation to the question of how to make sure that in taking these sound bytes, you weren't misquoting or manipulating to such a degree that the conclusion was foregone. So the first question is about formal procedures and obstacles you gave to yourself, and then the question of the ethics and aesthetics of collage.*

H. L. Hix: The process itself, in some ways, was simple. I just hired an assistant to download from www.whitehouse.gov all the public statements Bush made in his first term and convert the text into a word processing file. I printed this giant document—several thousand pages of tiny type—and simply read through it, a month's worth at a time, highlighter in hand. Then I would cut the highlighted passages and paste them into a smaller document, so that I had everything in one place. So the gathering part of it was very straightforward—just reading and reading, collecting what seemed relevant.

Once I started composing, the primary rule I set for myself was that I could juxtapose passages, but not leave things out silently. So any time there's a continuous passage with something that drops out, an ellipsis marks that it's been chopped in that way. Otherwise, I've allowed myself to take a passage from here and from there and put them together. I'm sure this results in various forms of distortion—how could it not?—but my thought was that this project was in some way like caricature, where distortion of features is intentional: "yeah, your nose isn't *that* big, but I drew it that big because it's a prominent part of your face." Even though the caricature is distorted, it's recognizable. Maybe, in a certain way, it's *more* accurate for the distortion. My objective was that sort of accuracy, that foregrounding of certain things. It's too easy to take anyone's words (Bush's words, or anyone's) and construct something just the opposite of what the speaker meant. I was interested in compressing things Bush said, putting together stuff said at different times but thematically connected, to test one statement by another. Political cartoons, a form of caricature, give one analogy for what I was up to.

I noticed that you used a number of poetic forms. One of the jokes of the book, in a sense, is that George Bush, a man who confesses his own inarticulateness, suddenly becomes someone speaking in sestinas, sonnets, ghazals. Particularly the ghazal, which is a kind of interesting choice. I got those jokes. I'm curious about your own process of discovery as a writer, as a result of the procedure. One thing that critics often say about political writing is that if the writer already knows the outcome, the reader will not be engaged either (Frost's "no surprise for the writer, no surprise for the reader"). What sort of surprises came to you as a result of the process?

Thanks for getting the joke of having Bush speak in a ghazal! I confess I felt smug for the rest of the day after coming up with that idea.

There were several surprises for me. One came out of my more or less arbitrary decision to write one poem per month of Bush's speeches. I made the decision for practical reasons: a month seemed likely to give enough material to construct a poem, and yet seemed somehow manageable. What I noticed, though, in simply reading through everything that happened in a given month, was how typically some theme asserted itself. Education and energy, for example, are frequent themes prior to 9/11.

Another surprise to me was the difference between the Bush and bin Laden poems. The Bush poems began first. I set myself rules for them, and expected, when I then decided I needed the bin Laden poems, that I'd use the same procedures to make the bin Laden poems I was using to make the Bush poems. But I found I couldn't. I took that as a revelation about both Bush's rhetoric and bin Laden's rhetoric, that one lends itself to a certain procedure, and the other does not. I don't think it was primarily because I was working in the original language with Bush and in translation with bin Laden, or that I had access to more material from Bush. It seemed to me primarily due to Bush's manner of speaking, which is very simple in its syntax and diction. It's very paratactic: little short declarations with no integral relationship to one other. They can be rearranged very easily—

Bush as the New Sentence.

Hah! Right!

Anything can happen after anything else.

Exactly. They do that in his prepared speeches. During the campaign, the time lead-ing up to the second election, when they're doing a lot of similar speeches, there's a lot of cutting and pasting going on. We're talking to this audience today, so we'll put these pieces together. It's more or less fungible material, without any integral relation of subordination, and no acknowledgment of logical consequence.

Just as, in a sense, your poems are authored by Bush, Bush is also authored by something else, some discourse. I got the sense not of Bush the man, but Bush the machinery of discourse. There is a wonderful and very scary talk poem by David Antin in which he talks about the Black Box as the operant metaphor for the way in which we view in the President a kind of omniscience or authority which is not tenable. Did you feel that...kind of character. Another way of saying this is that this book is not George Bush, but "My George Bush," like "My Emily Dickinson," Harvey Hix being possessed by Bush. Did you feel like he was getting inside your head, or at least feel the ghosts of logic haunting you?

Yes. Partly because the process was so intense. Insofar as *God Bless* is an occasional book—related to a specific set of events in history—there's a time period to it. It's part of another less visibly occasional project, one that I hope helps orient it toward history in a (relatively) timeless rather than a (merely) timely way. I've been working for a long time on the modest task of rewriting the Bible; for example, my longish poem "A Manual of Happiness," in *Surely As Birds Fly*, moves Job from ancient Pal-estine to modern Missouri and listens more to the seven sons and three daughters who get "disappeared" in the tale than to Job himself. When the whole Bible project is brought together, *God Bless* will serve as my Book of Kings. I hope that, just as the value of the biblical original was not confined to the time period in which the events occurred, so any value that inheres in *God Bless* will extend into the indefinite future.

Still, I knew the book had to happen in a certain time frame, so I worked on it very intensively: beyond my work obligations, all I read for four months was Bush. Night and day. I worked on the poems early in the morning and late at night. I imagine that reading anyone that compulsively—some marvelous literary figure, for instance—would make the author's voice part of the reader. It was an odd feeling. Definitely what you're talking about, a kind of speaking through, happened, a reci-procity between his words and my putting them together.

But it's complicated by the question about when his words *are* his words. If you read all the public statements, you see a major difference between what happens in a prepared speech, where someone has written it for him, where he's reading out what he's supposed to say, and what happens in a press conference, where he's off script and says whatever comes into his head. There's even a difference between a formal press conference, when he's at the podium with some leader from another country, and when he's in Crawford, intentionally being "down home," walking the reporters through the ranch. He works hard at fitting the discourse to the occasion, letting the occasion, the context, the needs of the audience heavily influence what he says and how he says it. I suppose we all do that, but it's very visible when you're President, when your words are performatives that alter history and end human lives.

So when you noticed this distinction, did you find the prepared speeches or the off-the-cuff remarks were more truthful for you, or were they both in play for you?

They both stayed in play throughout. I think all the poems ultimately involve both of them. But I felt I had to watch out for the off-the-cuff remarks, because they were where he would make his famous malapropisms, and I wanted to be wary of making things too fun, too easy. It wasn't the point, and there are plenty of people who can do that a lot better than I can. Bush does it himself; it's part of his persona that he can make fun of himself. I wanted there to be an aspect of humor to the book—some of the things he says are outrageous—but I was much more interested in the deadly serious side of it. I didn't want to focus too much on the off-the-cuff remarks: I wanted to attend to the prepared speeches also, and even such formal statements as proclamations.

In that sense, I think God Bless *is really not caricature, it's something else. It's poetry, and I think you should give yourself more credit than calling it caricature. The metaphor that came to my mind today was that you're sort of like an auto mechanic, and the car is discourse, and you're taking it apart, and looking at the parts, and then putting it back together. But in a sense, you're putting it back together in a new way, you're making it work. Maybe the discourse is a junk car, it's not going anywhere, and you're making it run again. What I found powerful about your procedure is that you're paying attention to his words, which to me is a very political thing to do. There's this idea in Slavoj Žižek, quoting Sloterdijk's critique of Cynical Reason—that the way to challenge or resist a discourse is not to take a cynical or ironic distance from it, but to take it completely at its word. That's exactly what the project does, you take it as its word. When you look at those words, you see them in a new way. So it's a really serious project.*

Definitely. One of the asymmetries between Bush and bin Laden is that bin Laden is paying very careful attention to Bush's words and actions. He may be interpreting them wrongly or overinterpreting, but he's paying very careful attention. In contrast, Bush is willfully *not* paying attention to bin Laden. Soon after 9/11, Bush is asked at a press conference whether he's seen the latest video message from bin Laden: Bush laughs it off, and says no, he didn't look at it. It's an astonishing moment, in which we've received a statement from the person who's claiming responsibility for an attack on our country, purporting to explain why it was done, and the President of our country is not willing to look at it?!? It's astonishing, and typifies a real asymmetry between the two. I was interested in playing the "paying attention" part, rather than the not paying attention part. Whatever the result may be.

The bin Laden poems are sort of more complicated poetically, but you're forced to reconstruct, in a sense, this other discourse, which you get in dribs and drabs, but obviously one of the critiques of those poems would be that you make fundamentally irrational ideology all too rational, you take the liberal self-critique to it, a la Christopher Hitchens, an irrational evil glomming onto historical grievances. Now I could take the exact opposite tack as well, that this is "My bin Laden," that you're trying to talk back to the Bush's voice as much as trying to represent bin Laden.

Just as there is an odd reciprocity between my voice and the Bush voice in the Bush poems, so too there's an odd reciprocity between my voice and the bin Laden voice in the bin Laden poems. The process is very different, using my words to recreate his arguments. But that means I'm making a lot of choices about the premises of the argument, what can be skipped, what seems plausible, and so on. So there's definitely an element of my voice there. That doesn't mean I advocate his views, but I do want to pay attention. One pays attention to the words of one's opponent. Even if it is one's enemy. Even if that enemy is evil. Out of self-interest, you still pay attention to their words, and try to see through the lies and understand the actual motives. One of the causes of the self-destructiveness of our policy decisions has been our refusal to do that work. We've substituted willful misattribution of motives to bin Laden, Hussein, al-Qaeda, etc., and we are suffering grievously the results of that willful inattention. Lumping them together is a mistake: their motives are not uniform, so the unwillingness to attend to what's being said—even if it's a lie, how are you going to see through the attempt to deceive if you're not paying attention to it?

There is a minor genre of poetry in which poets publish in poetry books political poems that they refuse to call poems, as in Denise Levertov's "Perhaps No Poem, But I Cannot Remain Silent." Talk about the decision to subtitle God Bless *a "Political/Poetic Conversation," and the attendant desire to add the critical apparatus of interviews to go with it.*

I identify with the refusal you refer to. I'm not sure how to speak in this time period, a time in which Kant's notion that we have to assume each other's honesty does not hold. We assume now that we are lying to one another, and that our speech is an attempt to coerce the other to advance our desires. Our representative speech act now is the advertisement; we take speech as inherently commercial. I'm interested in trying to figure out, in a society that has suspended our agreement that we be honest with each other, what it means to attempt to speak the truth. I'm not sure how one does that, how I might do that, so the book is a stab in the dark, taking speech that embraces its corruptness and putting it into poetic forms that purportedly arise from and exemplify an ideal of purity and integrity in speech.

As for the interviews, I'm aware that my expertise in these matters is very limited. I'm not an historian, I'm not a political scientist, I have no special expertise in these matters. My ambition is limited to being a responsible citizen in a democracy, a democracy premised upon dialogue and conversation, upon language use. There came a point in the process of working on the book, after I had entered into a dialogue with Phil Brady at Etruscan Press, that I felt I needed to draw in additional expertise I couldn't contribute myself. That was when I began to call on others who had some form of insight that wasn't being represented in the decision-making by the administration. Through the interview form, I could give myself and the book's readers access to these others' various forms of expertise.

One of the ways in which civilian writers have written about war is to employ documentary modes, either using documentary texts or adopting the neo-objective style of documentary cinematic. That's one of the things you do so well here, is write a poetry of the home front, something that our poetic canon has real difficulty locating and articulating.

The initial motivation for starting the project was to create a chronicle. I think you're right about the importance of documentary. C. D. Wright is teaching a course this semester on the documentary impulse in poetry, and I know I'm not the only poet who has felt obliged to respond to this administration, or the only poet who has arrived at the documentary mode as the closest thing to an antidote to, or an antibody against, this administration's toxins.

One thinks of Charles Reznikoff's Holocaust, *even though you're thinking about poetic form in a way that he wasn't.*

Yes, that sense of simply recording what has been. I was made more conscious that we receive public speech in extraordinarily fragmented form. Even someone who is more responsible than I normally am will likely hear at most a few lines from any one of Bush's speeches—and yet he's said all this stuff. I thought that what I could contribute was a block of time to read everything he said, and re-present through compression some element of the totality, so that all those interrelationships show up in a different way. One of the realizations I had was, omigod, he was talking about Iraq and "regime change" obsessively from the moment he took office. He didn't wait until after 9/11.

The poetry is historically textured in that way.

I know all of this is flavored by my own political predispositions. If I were The Decider, things would be different.... But my hope is that there's a strong element of simply reconstructing what was said, reminding ourselves of it, so that anyone, regardless of political predispositions, would find some insight as a result of this process. That's a way in which the project is intended to be more historical than occasional. We need ongoing testimony to past wounds: the Holocaust, Vietnam, et al. I want this book to take its place among the witnesses to the events of our time.

I wrote a poem some time before 9/11 called "Enemigos," that takes a Bush speech about the paranoia of the other, but after the terrorist attack, I was scared that maybe he was right, and that my liberal trust of others was naïve and misguided. When Colin Powell spoke in front of the United Nations about the dangers of Iraq, I felt as if I had to take it seriously, even though I had been working to end the economic sanctions against Iraq in the late 1990s, and knew that the country was in no position of being a military threat.

The fear they provoked put such pressure on discourse that everybody felt constrained in what they said. In this book, I asked whether a different kind of pressure could be placed on the discourse, a kind of opposite pressure. I don't know if it works or not.

I hope that Bush's actual voice could be spliced into your poems and done into an audio poem, in the form of the audio mash-up. Not as a parody of Bush, a Frankensteining of Bush, but as a form of reanimation.

I don't know if all the passages that exist as text exist as video or audio, so it may not even be possible, and certainly I don't have the technical know-how to make it happen myself, but it would be amazing to have that alternative Bush: the synthesized, synoptic presentation in opposition to the usual fragmented, excerpted presentation.

Why not call it poems? Why the hedging? What's your best argument for this as poetry?

I have to hedge on whether my attempt in this particular book *succeeds* in achieving its aims: readers will decide that for themselves. But I'd be much more assertive in declaring that its aims don't disqualify it from being poetry. Just because the book doesn't present in pretty words any epiphanies over sunsets or lamentations of lost love doesn't mean it's not poetry.

Poetry has shown a lot of flexibility across time and across cultures to do a lot of different work. What Adrienne Rich calls the "columnar, anecdotal, domestic poem" may be what we're most accustomed to recognizing as poetry in this time and this country, and it may be what's easiest to teach in a workshop setting, but "emotion recollected in tranquillity" is not the only thing poetry can do. Homer thought poetry could record and interpret war, Dante thought poetry could synthesize human knowledge, Milton thought poetry could justify the ways of God to man, the participants in the oral tradition that composed Job thought poetry could orient us metaphysically. I think poetry can interrogate political ideals and actions, can engage in thought and critique, can chronicle and question. I don't know if this book succeeds or not, but it's trying to do all those things.

A Conversation with John Poch

John Poch: *It's obvious by reading your criticism that philosophy and literary theory are important to you. It's obvious by reading your poetry that art and music shape your aesthetic. With so many interests that you take to heart by pursuing deeply, reading extensively, how does a singular book of poems take shape for you?*

H. L. Hix: For me the book is a more fundamental unit than the individual poem. Partly this is just getting and spending: I buy many books of poetry, but I subscribe to few journals, so the "unit" through which I most often gather poetry is the book. But it's more than that. My first acquaintance with contemporary poetry wasn't until graduate school: my undergraduate degree, from what was then a small college, left me with the impression that inspiration had ceased in England with Browning and in the U.S. with Whitman. For all I knew, being a poet was like being a tinker: they had 'em in the old days, but not any more. From my first awareness of more recent work, I loved books that tried to be more than "a heap of random sweepings": Merwin's *The Lice*, Ted Hughes' *Crow*, Berryman's *Dream Songs*. To this day, I tend to fall for books that are, or that I can read as, a single poem rather than a collection of discrete poems: C. D. Wright's *Deepstep Come Shining*, for example, or Claudia Rankine's *Don't Let Me Be Lonely*.

So for me the "architecture" of the book precedes the writing of the individual poems. It's not even that I write a few poems and early on develop a sense for a possible shape, which then gets filled out with more poems: the shape comes first, and only then the poems. The shape of the book usually changes radically over the course of its development, but there's always an "architecture," a "project," at the start of things.

Which is where the philosophy and art and music come in. I'm less interested in poetry as a means of "self-expression" than as a vehicle for exploring the human condition, of a piece with (rather than in contrast to) the sciences, philosophy, the other arts, and so on. My life history and my personality, the aspects of myself that are uniquely mine, seem to me less dramatic than the norm—more good fortune than bad, few personal tragedies (and none I'm not guilty of helping bring about), few lapses in personal safety and health, not rich, not poor. Not much to bind the attention of others. I accept such attentions gratefully, even greedily, when they are gifts motivated by the giver's friendship or love, but I don't see in my life history or personality any basis for exacting attention as tribute. My humanity, though, the aspect of myself that I share with others, is every bit as interesting as anyone else's. So I try to keep my life history and personality covert in and accidental to my poems, and to make my humanity—*our* humanity—overt and essential. That's one way of saying why the making public of poetry, its public-ation, doesn't make it feel to me any less intensely private. And why those other vehicles—philosophy, theory, art, music—pervade my poetry and help shape it.

In both your poetry and your criticism, you often have sections of epigrams/aphorisms mak-ing up a part of the book. Why are you attracted to this form of language and where do you draw the line between poetry and philosophical prose, if there is such a line?

My response to this will be a little like my response to the first question. Just as I am influenced by, and side with, those who don't assume that the self-enclosed short lyric confessional poem is somehow the standard for poetry, so I am influenced by, and side with, those who don't grant the deductive syllogism status as the pinnacle of reasoning. Plenty of philosophers, from Aristotle on, have been guided—produc-tively enough—by that ideal, but the pre-Socratics and Nietzsche and Wittgenstein wrote with some other norm in mind, a norm that invited them to more aphoristic writing.

I feel more welcomed as a reader into this aphoristic philosophy than into "syl-logistic" philosophy, more like a participant in a seminar and less like an auditor at a lecture. As a writer, I don't want to be the harrumphing codger, arms folded across his chest, condescending to the untutored masses who if they just knew a little more would see things my way. I'd much rather be leaning over the radiator with the au-thor when I'm reading, or with the reader when writing, both of us with wrenches in hand, mumbling and grunting as we try to piece things together.

The piecing of things together may be the point of connection between my response to the first question and my response to the second. I don't think of life as something that's dark until one finds the light switch, finds the syllogism or lyric in-sight that will suddenly illuminate the whole. There's something more apt in a Lego metaphor: we're constantly having experiences that need assimilation, experiences whose relation to previous experience is not given or self-evident, always inviting assembly and re-assembly. In the light-switch metaphor, one truth illuminates once and for all, but there's no once-and-for-all quality to the Legos. There's always more assembly to be done.

Do you consider yourself a "philosopher"? Is this term any more difficult to take on than that of "poet"?

There's a stronger tradition, I'd say, of combining the practice of philosophy with the practice of fiction writing than of combining philosophy with poetry. A person practicing both philosophy and fiction has Camus and Sartre to look to, and Iris Murdoch, and more recently William Gass, Lars Gustafsson, Lynne McFall, and no doubt others I'm not thinking of at the moment. But what poets have formal training in philosophy? There's T. S. Eliot, of course, and among our contemporaries Jan Zwicky (whose work, by the way, is very important to me) and Troy Jollimore and John Koethe. But I'm not aware of many others.

Surely many practices open possibilities for inquiring into and attempting to understand our humanity. I've chosen philosophy and poetry, but I would practice more than just those two if I could manage it: I wish I could figure out how to be a mathematician, too, and a cellist and a sculptor and a botanist… It has seemed important to me to try to maintain active inquiry through more than one practice, by analogy with binocular vision, hoping that the two practices, philosophy and poetry, will work together to create a conceptual "depth perception," the way a person's two eyes work together to create sensual depth perception. I've published more in the field of poetry, but so far I've taught more philosophy courses than creative writing courses.

You're right, though, about both terms being difficult to take on. Both practices invite pretension: I've known at least as many smug philosophers as self-aggrandizing poets, and no doubt I'm guilty myself. But I try to pay double attention to Louise Glück's maxim that "'Poet' must be used cautiously; it names an aspiration, not an occupation." The same warning might usefully be made about the name "philosopher."

But maybe this answer's starting to drift. The short, direct response is, yes, even though I'm wary of the assertion of essence implied by "poet" and "philosopher," I do still consider myself fully engaged in the practice of poetry *and* fully engaged in the practice of philosophy.

See what I mean? Even after saying yes, you qualify it. It's hard to take on those titles.

If this were a cocktail party, I'd be perfectly comfortable saying I'm a poet, or saying I'm a philosopher. There you'd be asking just to be polite, and all I'd be telling you is I'm not a surgeon or a garbage collector or a senator. Here, though, your question's partly rhetorical, asserting a healthy skepticism: Do you *really* think you're a *philosopher?* At the cocktail party, your question would be about me, what I do for a living; here, the question is really about the categories of "poet" and "philosopher." The question isn't treating those titles as occupational designations but as honorifics. The subtext isn't, "Why are you wearing a turtleneck and a sport jacket instead of a suit and tie?", it's more like, "Do you think you deserve a place among the Worthies?" *That* I'm nervous about, and feel compelled to qualify!

This morning I was reading an interview of Lisa Robertson in the current *Denver Quarterly*, in which she gives an interesting reply to a similar question. Robertson says, "I am not as interested in writing 'poems' as I am in continuing to participate in a fabric of intellectual life and relationship…. Poetry is the frame of my engagement with the world, not the substance of it." I wish I'd said that.

You've written prose text for a few art catalogues and you used to work as vice president of academic affairs for the Cleveland Institute of Art. Can you talk a bit about how the visual and the verbal intersect in the best poetry? And in art?

I feel fortunate to have "grown up" among visual artists at the Kansas City Art Institute and the Cleveland Institute of Art. Part of what I learned from my colleagues at those two colleges has to do with the *practice* of an art. My studio colleagues model, for instance, an *immersion* in their work that I find inspiring. Next time you feel stalled out in your writing, figure out a way to spend a couple of hours with the artist China Marks. It's not just that she's always *thinking* about her work, though she *is* always thinking about it, but that she's involved in the work, submerged in it, as a whole person: her mind, senses, spirit, her whole body. I feel moved, transported, every time I'm with her, overcome by her *urgency*.

But maybe that gives me a way to square up to your question more directly. For me, the intersection of visual and verbal hasn't been conjunction so much as analogy. In other words, it's not primarily that I've tried to mix the two (though my poems are often ekphrastic, at least in origin, and of course I always want the imagery to be effective). Instead, I feel that my attention to the qualities of poetry has been trained by what my colleagues have taught me about the qualities of visual art. I'll never forget asking Carl Kurtz about his peculiar set of passions: calligraphy (his studio practice), but also ballet and drag racing. His answer had to do with totality of purpose: every element of a dragster is designed and assembled to make it go faster for a quarter mile in a straight line, and there's a similar conspiracy of detail and completeness of synthesis and insistence of craft in the composition of one of Carl's calligraphic pieces. I want my poems, like his visual work, to have that quality.

In As Easy as Lying, *you spend a decent amount of time traversing the "seemingly" disparate poles most commonly called "New Formalism" and "L=A=N=G=U=A=G=E Poetry" or the "Avant Garde." You are severely critical of books by Jarman and Ashbery, yet praise Gioia and Bernstein. What aspect of each group/school do you find most appealing? Beyond the fiction of "schools," which poets do you find using the best of both worlds?*

Insofar as the fiction of schools has any value—and I think you're right to call it a fiction—that value seems to me to lie in its provoking critical thought. Members of a school spend time and energy defining the school by genus and species, placing it within a tradition (the genus part) and distinguishing it from—asserting its superiority over—other contemporary approaches (the species part). So, of schools themselves, I'm most interested in the theorizing. The results of L=A=N=G=U=A=G=E poetry, for instance, that have mattered most to me have been the critical works. Lyn Hejinian's *The Language of Inquiry* is very important to me, as have been all of Charles Bernstein's essay collections, and Leslie Scalapino's *Syntactically Impermanence*, and others. It's not that I think any one school is better than another, but that I'm interested in the way rationales for the superiority of schools help to identify and clarify value judgments about poetry that otherwise we tend to make without thinking them through.

In theorizing, I'm interested in the thesis and antithesis; in poetry per se (I say this knowing that contrasting "poetry per se" to theorizing is tendentious and misleading), I'm more engaged by synthesis, by work that seems to have assimilated various conceptual frames, and to manifest an identity that resists resolution into or identification with something that antedates it.

In part, I'm sure this preference of mine—which I put forward only as a preference, with no insinuation that others ought to share it—comes from a sense I have about the practice of poetry. Probably I shouldn't even say "the" practice of poetry. I find that in my own attempt to practice poetry, there's an alternation between conscious and unconscious, reflection and projection. I find it important to *think* about poetry, to try to understand what I'm doing and why I'm doing it, but I also find that this happens mostly as rationalization, after the fact. I construct a few paragraphs of theory as a way of reconciling myself to what I've been doing in lines.

By looking back and looking around, I try to make conscious what has been unconscious in me. I start acting differently, though, when I reframe my past actions. Refiguring what I have done reconfigures what I want to do. It's not that I start writing poetry primarily as a conscious activity or to prove a theory—god forbid!—but that a new consciousness changes what is happening unconsciously.

In God Bless, *your quirky critique and poetical response to our recent decade of war and terror in the Middle East (and also a dialogue with a host of writers/thinkers), you confront the failure of both Bush and bin Laden to see an(other) perspective. The poems could be categorized as "found" poems in that you cobbled together various quotations by these men to form villanelles, sonnets, ghazals, etc. Right after the poems, in the first interview, there seems an admission to the possibility of dishonesty through re-contextualization. What were your doubts and beliefs in this work as it proceeded? And where is H. L. Hix (your language and voice) in all this?*

It's different enough from anything I've done before that I worried throughout the process about what in the world I was doing. I had belief enough to see the project through—or energy enough, or obstinacy enough. But, as your question intuits, I had plenty of doubts, too.

Still, I think the found-ness and collage-ness of the work doesn't make me any less present in it than in anything else I've written, and I hope the work questions assumptions about poetry that would suggest otherwise. For one thing, I want to assert that "emotion recollected in tranquillity" may suggest something about some poetry but is by no means an exhaustive definition, or a universally applicable one. It might be adequate to lying on one's couch in vacant or in pensive mood, recalling a host of golden daffodils, but it doesn't address *The Iliad*'s immersion in history and social identity and the inexorability of forces larger than ourselves, or Job's struggle with the grating of what is over what ought to be. In *God Bless*, I'm not trying to recollect my emotion, so I'm not in the poem in that way, but that doesn't keep me from being in the poem as a citizen of a belligerent nation, fretting the causes and effects of that belligerence, deformed by my complicity in it.

To put this another way, I suspect that the poetic imagination might manifest itself in any number of ways, not only by "making things up." By comparison to prose, I'd say that *God Bless* is more like nonfiction than like fiction. Or by comparison to other media, I'd appeal to documentary film. Ken Burns and Jane Campion aren't doing the same thing, but I wouldn't describe either director as being more present in his/her films. In most of my work, I'm probably after something more like what Campion does, but in *God Bless*, I'm being more like Burns.

In all honesty, I have to say that I'm skeptical of exactly how much can be achieved socially through poetry. In a country of over three hundred million, if a poet sells over one thousand books, she is deemed a success. Isn't Auden right when he says in "In Memory of W.B. Yeats," "Poetry makes nothing happen." Throughout his own writing, Auden insisted even more so than Yeats on that differentiation between rhetoric and poetry. But then, despite his accusation that Yeats' was "silly" (probably referring to his political work that did nothing but leave Ireland with "her madness and her weather still") that mercury falling in the thermometer at the beginning of this poem is transformed, by the end, into "the healing fountain" issuing from the human heart. It seems to me that Auden hopes something can happen personally through poetry if it is given a human voice to "say" it, but social change?

In one sense, I share your skepticism. I'm not expecting a call from President Bush saying he's read my book and he's going to do things differently from now on, or an article in the *Times* about the national groundswell of support my book has provoked for more pacific foreign policy.

But I think there's another angle on this, too. I want to distinguish between two kinds of activism, one I'd call coercive and one I'd call persuasive. Both are needed, but they operate differently. Coercive activism operates on the *effects* of power relations. Strikers don't expect to change management's mind about the rights of laborers; they want to cut the cord between current treatment of laborers and the profit of management. The "argument" in a strike is: keep treating us badly and you'll lose money; you'll turn a profit only if you treat us differently; you don't get what you want until we get what we want. Persuasive activism operates on the *causes* of power relations. Management treats labor badly partly because it awards itself greater entitlement than labor to goods and privileges. The "argument" in a poem (or other vehicle of persuasive activism) is that you should reconsider—and change—the valuations on which you base your actions.

I suspect poetry can *support* coercive activism (as when strikers unite in chanting or singing verse), but whether or not it is supporting coercive activism poetry can itself only engage in persuasive activism. It's one way to make sense of "poetry makes nothing happen": poetry cannot coerce, cannot withhold capital from the greedy. However, it may persuade; that is, it may alter the value judgments from which the greed of the greedy derives, so liberating the greedy to be other than greedy.

I do have to say that I am persuaded, at times, that poetry can function, in some small way, to bear witness and raise awareness and call us to action. When I read a book such as Peter Balakian's The Black Dog of Fate, *I come to the understanding that his poems about the*

Armenian genocide DO something. But then I get skeptical again, because I see that maybe it's not the poems, but the memoir and Balakian's tireless activism that gets the word out. I wonder about God Bless *in this way. What would these poems be without the interviews at the end? And seriously, how many copies of* God Bless *have been bought and read? Aren't most poets overly romantic in the way we believe our work matters? I mean, it matters deeply to me and to you, but to the world?*

I wish *God Bless* would alter U.S. foreign policy, but you're right that it's doomed to total failure if that's the only criterion for its value. I don't think it's sold any more copies than the usual hilariously tiny number of copies my books sell. It may not be a legislator, but it's certainly unacknowledged! But poetry isn't *only* about effecting social change; it's also about personal and civic integrity. It can be a way of "going on record." In committee meetings, I'm often in the minority on an item of debate, and sometimes the circumstances are such that I want to go on record as opposing an action taken. I do so not with the expectation that it will have any *effect* at all, but simply from perceived obligation. Similarly, though I don't anticipate my book having any effect on public policy, I nevertheless felt obligated to write it, to go on record. It doesn't release me from complicity in the actions of my government, but it complicates that complicity.

This could also be stated by noting the value we attribute to minority opinions in law. We consider the formulation of the minority opinion in Supreme Court cases important, but not because it changes the decision at all, or changes who the decision affects. I think of *God Bless* as something like a minority opinion. I'm influenced here by Iris Murdoch, whose argument in *The Sovereignty of Good* asserts, in the terms of your question, that something's mattering deeply to you and to me might impose obligation, even if attending to the obligation has no effect at all on others, or on one's own circumstances.

As for the interviews, I don't worry about their worth: they were *very* interesting to conduct, and the interviewees have important things to say. I do worry about the relationship between the interviews and the poems. In a very smart essay in *Pleiades*, David Caplan criticizes my inclusion of the interviews as too explanatory. He's probably right that, by making the project more palatable to a wider potential audience, publishing the interviews in the same book also normalizes, and so weakens, the poems.

Well, if I may argue in your defense, What doesn't explain a book of poems? The cover, the blurbs, the press that publishes it, the author photograph, even snazzy introductions by Robert Pinsky or some other institution: all these "explain." I haven't read Caplan's essay, but I'd argue that your inclusion of the interviews is a much more interesting "explanation."

It's a tough balance to hit. How much of the apparatus is helpful welcome for a reader entering a complex text, how much is greasy salesmanship, how much is valid teamwork with the publisher (who, after all, has to sell books to stay afloat), how much is condescension to a reader perfectly capable of "getting it" without being told what's going on? At least with the interviews, I do feel that they have independent validity, whatever their relationship to the poems.

Now that I think about it, most of your books try to bridge territories that most folks would rather separate: Poetry/Philosophy, Postmodernism/New Formalism, Poetry/Politics, Poetry/Music, Poetry/Religion, and even Christianity/Islam. You seek out commonalities rather than differences. Beyond commonalities, harmony might be the right word. Would it be safe to say that this is the thrust or mission of your work?

Harmony, definitely. Though with emphasis on a particular aspect of harmony, namely the tension in it, the reconciliation of opposition. It's a religious urge for me, the wish for what in Christian terminology gets called redemption; it's social, reflecting my admiration for citizenship like that of Jimmy Carter, with all his efforts toward reconciling conflicts between nations; it's existential, an attempt to reconcile myself to the multiplicities and incoherences of my life.

For me this harmonizing of tensions is a metaphysical concern. I'm skeptical of the Cartesian premise that the cosmos is unified in such a way that in principle complete Truth is available to us: Descartes thinks if we would just work together and if we had enough time, we could know everything, and when we did we'd be seeing one integrated whole. My guess is that Heraclitus was getting warmer: "Nature loves to hide"; "Humans deceive themselves about the apparent..."; "...a thing is homologous by difference from itself; its harmony is tensile, like that of the bow and the lyre."

It's also a psychological concern, reflecting the aspect of inner experience that such pre-neurology psychologists as Plato and Freud portrayed metaphorically. I'm thinking of the charioteer in the *Phaedrus*, the soul depicted as two willful and untamed horses yoked together. Or the id and superego butting heads. My primary interest is not, like neurologists, in identifying the genetic basis or locating the neuronal event-site of internal conflict, but in describing what the experience of internal conflict *feels like* and what it *means*, and exploring ways in which movement toward reconciliation might be possible. Camus famously described suicide as the only philosophical problem. I might say it slightly differently: it is by no means self-evident to me how to live with myself. Poetry is one of the ways in which I try to figure that out.

Certain commonalities don't harmonize. For instance, Bush's view that God is directing him and bin Laden's view that God is directing him. I suppose we have to find those things in Islam we admire (devotion, reverence, discipline) and even the commonalities we have with the Bush Administration. I mean, most people believe in the idea of "just war," but I hardly hear of anyone going back to Aquinas and Augustine to measure how far we might have strayed from their ideals. Are our military leaders investigating this? Our citizens? Our poets?

The interviewees in *God Bless* certainly are. Asma Afsaruddin works hard to go back to the Islamic siblings of Aquinas and Augustine, to remind us that extremism is anomalous in Islam, both historically and demographically. Mary Habeck and Peter Bergen identify points of commonality between the Bush administration and those of us with more liberal sensibilities. Paul Woodruff measures current Christianity (and other religions) against an earlier religious ideal in *Reverence*, and current democratic practice against democracy's earliest ideals in *First Democracy*.

In your most recent collection due out this fall, Legible Heavens, *the work in the section "Synopsis" arises from your readings of the gospels and other apocryphal works. Each poem seems to take its own approach in "translating" a particular passage of scripture. By the end, the lines seem to have gotten quite personal, making the voice of the Apostle James your own, saying "I, Harvey...solicit a miracle." What were your most surprising discoveries in doing this work? What is it within you that wants a miracle?*

I spend a lot of effort *denying* self-expression, confession, autobiography, and certain other vehicles of the personal any place in my poetry, but not because my poetry is not personal. I just want to construe the "personal" differently. For me, the metaphysical *is* personal. The conceptual or theoretical is personal. So you're right that the writing of that sequence was very personal, even though the poems are "translations" or "appropriations" of gospel passages and narratives.

   I was surprised to discover—or to be reminded—how much power the mythos or lexicon of the gospels retains for me, though I stopped *believing* any of it many years ago. I suspect we all want a miracle. The realistic side of me, the side that knows better than to watch for a miracle, wrote "A Manual of Happiness," my retelling of the book of Job, one take on the brute fact that the world is not arranged to fulfill our needs and desires, is not as we wish it were. "Synopsis" is its obverse, written by the side of me that holds out irrational hope, that still watches for miracles, or reads experiences as miracles, brute fact be damned. If Job stares down brute fact; the gospels peer around it.

I'm particularly interested in the mode of acknowledging the brute fact that contrasts faith to belief, rather than conjoining them. It's the mode of Unamuno's *San Manuel Bueno, Martyr*, of Kierkegaard, of Simone Weil's positing of *dis*belief as a criterion for the purity of faith when she suggests that one pray with the thought that God does not exist, and reminds us that "we are subject to that which does not exist." That's one subject/subjection I worry in "Synopsis."

Yet Job, perhaps the oldest text in the Scriptures, seems to be a very New Testament kind of book. Not the ending, where he gets everything back (which to me seems beside the point), but the fact that God admires Job's brutal honesty and condemns the "friends" who seem to be quoting directly out of the Psalms/Proverbs, saying, You reap what you sow. Job is a book of grace in that way, like the gospels. Jesus objects to "religion" just as Job's God does.

The ending is a late addition to a work that seems to me much more interesting without it. The redactor who added the ending wanted to preserve deuteronomic theology, denial of which is pretty obviously the point of the rest of the poem. So I get what you mean about the similarity between the God of Job and the God of the gospels. You don't have to look around to see that in this world good does not consistently follow good or bad always follow bad. If grace is to come to us, it will come as, well, *grace*, rather than as reward that God's contracted to, that we can claim. God, or the demiurge, or the cosmos: put in the way you just put it, Socrates and his pals in the *Republic* search for grace no less urgently than Job and Jesus do.

You do a lot of wrestling with God/god/the gods/the lack thereof. And you admit to being somewhat of a nihilist? Where are you, personally, in this struggle and where do you see it going?

It *is* a struggle for me, partly due to personal history. I was raised in a Southern Baptist household that took its religion very seriously, and I myself was earnest enough that as an undergraduate I was licensed (the first step toward becoming a Southern Baptist minister), though I was never ordained (the second and conclusive step). But now I'm the only person, I think, in my extended family—on either side, as far as the eye can see: grandparents, aunts, uncles, cousins, nieces and nephews—who does not identify with, practice, or at least accede to some version of fundamentalist Christianity. I absorbed a lot of the values espoused by that household (respect for others, tempering of self-interest by the interests of others, etc.), but the purported facts that, for the others in my family, ground the values (there's a beneficent God who cares about individual humans, and so on) now appear to me to be wish-fulfillments, obviously false. So—since we've been talking about the personal—a number of basic spiritual and philosophical problems (Why should I be good? Why do humans suffer? and so on) feel very *personal* to me. I inherited from my religious upbringing a sense I can't quite shake, that—like it or not—one's very life is staked on how one answers metaphysical questions and projects oneself ethically.

That's another take on what I was trying to get at earlier in backgrounding life history and foregrounding humanity. There's not much in my life history to depict by way of events: no emotional or physical abuse, no overcoming of addiction, no perilous youthful sowing of wild oats, no struggle for survival in a war-torn city. Good little boy becomes black sheep of family. Ho hum. Yet the situation I take myself to share with all other humans feels wildly dramatic: lives, including my own, hang in the balance. That probably also explains why my numerous attempts at fiction all have failed. I don't feel conflict most deeply through *event*, but through *situation*.

Wish fulfillments, you say. But just because someone wishes something doesn't make it false.

Granted. So I should correct myself by saying that many of the propositions asserted by fundamentalist Christianity appear to me to be wish fulfillments *and* to be obviously false. These range from literal interpretations of narratives that appear to me to be figurative (the sun stopping for a day), to conceptual notions I find utterly implausible (a beneficent and omnipotent deity requires a blood sacrifice to be appeased for perceived wrongs; a human sacrifice alleviates guilt of yet-unborn persons; etc.). I still draw heavily on those funds, but for different purchase. The fallen condition of humanity once helped me manage my sense of dependence, explaining why membership in a particular community assured me of a future well-being that others could not expect; now it helps me deal with my complicity in issues larger than myself (my enjoying the benefits of citizenship in a nation that harms and exploits other nations, my receiving a salary from a state treasury filled mostly through massive ecological irresponsibility, and so on).

You write in As Easy as Lying *that "Belief suffocates imagination." The word "suffocate" seems rhetorical here. You could have easily said, "Imagination suffocates belief," no? Can't we have both?*

I'm sure you're right that we can—and probably must—have both. But my apothegm, for all its hyperbolic rhetoric, its condensation of the "big" issues of belief and imagination we've just been talking about, is probably after something fairly modest, a preference for the provisional over the final, for process over conclusion, for exploration over conviction, originary over derivative, discovered over imposed, and so on.

You direct the creative writing program at the University of Wyoming. In your experience, what is the most important role of a director?

As we speak, my appointment to the directorship is nearing its end (it was a three-year term, and my colleague Beth Loffreda will now step in to direct the program for the next term). I have felt as my first responsibility the enabling of *community*. I mean by that something very straightforward. In workshop or out, the teaching of writing depends heavily on dialogue, and dialogue depends on the people engaged in it: the knowledge and perspective they bring to the dialogue, but also the goodwill, mutual trust, common purpose, respect, and commitment. I count myself fortunate to be part of an MFA that really is a community, made of people with diverse backgrounds but with shared goodwill, who are deeply engaged with one another's work.

I figure that in those conditions, surrounded by a bunch of very smart and energized writers (faculty and students alike), my "leadership" will consist mostly in *not* meddling. So we're very clear about the professor's autonomy, for instance. It's not for me to try to "manage" or regularize how workshops are taught, or even enforce that they be taught *as* workshops. If Alyson Hagy, wondering one semester whether fiction writing might best be taught by learning to line dance, were to hold her "workshop" at a local country/western bar, my job would be to share the students' surprise and trust, not to tell Alyson she has to make everybody sit down once a week around a conference table in the classroom building. I think of directing these writers as a little like caddying for Tiger Woods. Things are not going to go better if I try to tell him how to swing. They're going to go best if I walk beside him down the fairway and hand him the four iron when he asks for it.

But that makes my approach to directing the MFA at Wyoming sound more magnanimous and less self-interested than it's been. Really, I've just tried to follow Roethke's advice: "Surround yourself with rising waters: the flood will teach you to swim."

Letters to Jan Zwicky

December 2002

Because I worry about what poetry is,
    and am willing now to admit
that my poems like letters have an audience
    of one, because I want to speak
with a plainness I have not believed in before
    and do not trust yet to say what
I mean, or what the words themselves purport to say,
    you get this, my indecision
manifest, one part plain speech one part poetic,
    a letter that cannot quite trust
itself to be a poem, or not to be one,
    gray lines from a mind and a life
that stare each other down, but share now no language,
    no future, nothing in common,
and speak the way a feuding couple speaks,
    to each other but through a third.

That absolute separation of mind from life,
    of desire from obligation,
understanding from inertia, means I love
    much more than I can hold at once,
trust what I know as a lie more than what purports
    to be truth, and worship only
a god who does not exist, who speaks in riddles,
    who commands disobedience.
It means you were right to observe how intimate
    my abstractions are, those notes that
sound a spirit sundered utterly from any
    elements of experience,
closest to integrity where it stands farthest
    from reality, drawing me
to savor self-contempt in self-destructive acts
    that once I could not imagine.

So, yes, send more on silence and being unfit,
    for unfit I am and silent
I should be, since this sounds like grief that is in fact
    a spilling-out from one broken
by too much joy, filled too full of love, one trying
    from his infinite gratitude
to be what he is not (husband, teacher, leader),
    one who shares so insatiably
what you call your "huge appetite for solitude"
    that he has left even himself,
and now scatters small formalities like birdseed,
    hoping only briefly to see,
to tempt a few timid hungry fragments of his
    fugitive brightly-colored life.

March 2003

1.
Or as Oppen says it, *Each of us knows only*
    one thing for himself, and says that
in the poems. Canetti: *The philosopher*
    is known by the tiny number
of his chief ideas, and the stubborn, irksome way
    in which he reiterates them.
Maybe unknowability is an eros,
    an urge to pass beyond the world
compassed by return to oneself. Maybe others
    content within that world find things
knowable, articulable, satisfying.
    What then makes *our* eros virtue?

2.
Can one avoid serving a spiritual pose?
    What makes thinking superior
to giving up on the struggle? (Rest, after all,
    serving as the final telos

for Buddhists and Augustine.) The perplexity
        is not just about who one is—
that would set it limits, make possible a map.
        Our loneliness is infinite.
3.
It's an appealing category: *big* mistakes.
        One aspect of an ambition.
I want to make big mistakes, yes, but big mistakes
        that are generous, forgiving.
George Bush is making a big mistake now: a vain,
        greedy, irreverent mistake,
unlike the big mistake Simone Weil elected.
        What validates my preference,
though, for Weil's big mistake over Bush's? Nothing,
        unless some value can exist
wholly independent of ultimate value,
        which I doubt. (Read: prefer to doubt.)

4.
And what makes it good that we're trying to come home
        to ourselves? Even if we *are*
selves, and even if those selves are homes, why not try
        to leave them, the journey often
serving us as an affirmative metaphor.
        If we treat knowledge as fragrance—
lovely thought, for which thanks—we don't so much seek home
        as fall toward some flowering.

5.
Except there is no plain attention. I take that
        as one thing we mean by eros.
Surely plain attention would have to be open,
        not proscribed by self-interest,
but no human brain is capable of acting
        in that way, perception (through smell
no less than sight) operating by exclusion,

and perception serving as one
component of attention. We are brought at best,
    I think, *toward* plain attention,
but even that means moving away from ourselves,
    defying or overwhelming
neurology, which must be more like a trellis
    than a ladder that can be stored.

6.
The suspicion we might be crazy for feeling
    the erotic pull of meaning
comes (I think) from the surprise that you say you want
    to understand, but can't. Of course.
Because understanding is how we treat systems.
    We weep for Kierkegaard's reasons:
because understanding would imply communion
    with others, with language, with earth,
but eros entails isolation, estrangement,
    signals imminent tragedy.

7.
Certain phrases draw me: "unkink luminously,"
    "desire that both weakens and feeds,"
"glacially slow ravishment," "to be erotic
    and a failure." Certain phrases
attract me, but the whole is too much, as always.
    Which may count as explanation
for my philosophical dis-ease: I once felt
    I could embrace the whole: I felt
"saturated with intellectual purpose."
    Now I feel as a young girl must
tracing the thunderbird tattooed on a boy's back
    with her index finger. Weeping.

8.

Yes, *that* must be why true love is self-destructive,
    and is so necessarily.
If the language of system, itself a system,
    distorts moments of attention,
then either I lie any time I speak my love,
    or I cannot speak love at all.
Either way, veracious erotic attention
    will not join me to my beloved,
but—with finality—separate me from her.
    The more intensely I attend
the more decisively am I made alien
    from the object of attention.

9.

Not knowing where desire will go is not a state
    we should elect, but one we can't
escape, the state all our human institutions
    try to repress, much to our harm.
We marry as if desire were for one person,
    worship as if it were for good,
study as if desire were for the rational,
    and rule as if it meant to live.
"Erotic correction" can only cause exile,
    forty days in the wilderness,
waking in the middle of life in a dark wood,
    more receptive to beauty, yes,
but overwhelmed, too, by the irretrievable
    loss of every human love.

10.

Rain singing against slate shingles. Cars hissing past.
    The first thunder of the season.
It would be enough, except there is someone else
    in the rocking chair beside me.

11.

The first stepping-outside takes more naiveté
  than courage. You step out because
you can't see far enough ahead to know the door
  will shut behind you. Stepping out
may not demand a physical change in your life,
  but there is a reason mystics
lived in solitude: stepping outside abandons
  any other obligation.
Abandon any hope of being virtuous
  or whole all ye who exit here.

12.

Asking the difference between self-indulgence
  and eros assumes there is one,
assumes there is—there could be—some state not self-
  indulgent, a premise I doubt.
Dilemma has been for me not a starting point
  from which I escape, but the end
into which I am driven inexorably.
  I retreat by abandoning
those to whom I could fulfill my obligations
  only by deserting myself.
I indulge my sense of responsibility
  or my libido or my wish
for respectability or my vanity,
  but in any case I indulge.

13.

I claim it, the work of disorientation,
  as mine, though by definition
(and perhaps some other forms of necessity)
  I don't know how to fulfill it.
One day of snowmelt leaves me to dream of summer,
  of windows open overnight,
of being awakened long before dawn by crows
  enforcing hoarse hostilities.

14.

Not so simple, I think, as men define themselves,
        women are defined by others,
but that squared: men think they can (or even that they must)
        control how others define them,
women think allowing others to define them
        is an act of definition.
Eros divides by gender, but in so many
        more ways it eremites us all.

15.

For duty, conscience. What capacity of mind
        serves the same function for desire?

16.

This is where Kant went wrong: responsibility
        is not rational. Instinctive,
maybe, or sensual, or (your term) erotic,
        or simply imaginary.
I am responsible toward my wife because
        the sun that rose after I did
a month ago rises before me now. I bear
        responsibility toward
my colleagues because the tulips in the greenhouse
        have bloomed scarlet and lavender,
toward the rain forests because the density
        of unknown things there beckons me,
toward the future to cover for past failures,
        toward myself because why not.

17.

Nothing makes sense. And it would be impossible
        for anything *not* to make sense.
Only because we are talking have we been fooled
        into believing what we need
is to *talk* about "the simultaneity

of being erotically
impelled and caught in a large ethical labor."
        What we need is to survive it.

18.

After so much talk of responsibility,
        forgive my failure to fulfill
the one Kierkegaard imposes: *I can die, but
        I must not become tired.* Like Weil,
I love *everything*, and am borne down upon by
        "correspondingly enormous"
responsibility, only I lack her will.
        All of us carry infinite
responsibility. She and twenty more in
        history have lived up to it.
Weil's was *not* a misunderstanding, not failure.
        This is the sense of martyrdom:
we are responsible for more than what we do,
        so duty calls to death, not life.

19.

Discernment as pharmakon, administered to
        ward off vanity but serving
actually as the agent of infection,
        introducing self-interest
into ascesis, corrupting exactitude.
        I wish I, too, lacked discernment.

20.

We keep orbiting the same problem: if one can
        never say what most needs saying,
then like Weil we have no one to talk to. Our need
        to talk is not thereby relieved,
as witness your extensive dialogue and this
        palaver, my gloss, which leaves me
where you started me, at eros, urgency sired
        by poverty, borne by beauty.

July 2003

My thanks, as always, for your (lovely, as always)
    letter, and for its kind concern,
but be assured that what you take for exhaustion
    and skepticism is neither,
only my stuttering, my failure yet to find
    the right rhythm for the right words.
I work hard, yes, but others work as hard for less
    reward and less recognition,
so exhaustion would be for me not physical
    but moral weakness. Nor am I
skeptical, any more than the authors of *Job*
    and *Lear* are skeptical. Is it
skeptical to hear god in thunder, to create
    a character who says, "As flies
to wanton boys are we to the gods, they kill us
    for their sport"? You're right to observe
between what I say and what's happening to me
    a gap, but not one I would name
despair. Why not rather ecstasy that I find
    my own life less interesting,
less salient than other aspects of the world?
    Or a version of Kantian
detachment that finds all things—*all* things—beautiful.
    True, my world is nihilistic:
it seems to me self-evident—clear and distinct—
    that the universe offers us
no metaphysical foundation for value,
    but that to me seems less a cause
for despair than for defiance, for asserting
    value, for imagining it.
Of course there is much I can't say, now or ever.
    But I write to you from Ireland,
from a town on Connemara whose name I can't
    recall (it starts with R), looking

east across a bay as the sun sets behind me
    at eleven, at a landscape
that represents my world as well as anything,
    calm water, the peninsula
on the other side growing heavy underneath
    its eight white houses that hoard light
and float. I envy you your three (three!) instruments;
    maybe I will seek a teacher
and re-commence my struggles with the damned guitar.
    As for flowers, our salvia
and roses were doing well when we left. Iris
    an artist friend sent from Holland
were breathtaking two weeks ago. Please keep sending
    letters when you want to and can.

November 2003

Metaphor. To bear across. Or be borne across,
    I'd say, the passive voice standing
in this case closer to my own experience.
    To be borne across: my desire
(to use my blunter term), my eros (to borrow
    your more refined one). I think, though,
my preoccupations stray in one way from yours.
    Your gestalt of wisdom (read this
assertion, like all assertions in this letter,
    as a question) is and is not
metaphysics. Your wisdom sees and does not see
    the world. Such wisdom seems to me
attainable, at least in some portion. I see
    the world with force enough to keep
in check my not seeing it, to create, between
    my seeing and my not-seeing,
dynamic, gravid tension. I am overwhelmed
    by the world. I recognize it
and recognize myself in it. But my gestalt

of wisdom is inflected by
(and as) ethics: to recognize the human world.
    To see and not see in others
a recognition of the world I recognize.
    Here, though, no seeing balances
my not-seeing. Though I recognize myself as
    an inhabitant of the world,
I do not recognize myself as in a world
    shared by and with other humans.
That is my skepticism. I am not afraid
    the world may not exist but that
I may be alone in the world, that others may
    live in another world than mine.

About the Author

H. L. Hix teaches at the University of Wyoming and lives in Laramie.

Books from Etruscan Press

Etruscan Press is Proud of Support Received From

Wilkes University

Youngstown State University

The Raymond John Wean Foundation

The Ohio Arts Council

The Stephen & Jeryl Oristaglio Foundation

The Nathalie & James Andrews Foundation

The National Endowment for the Arts

The Ruth H. Beecher Foundation

The Bates-Manzano Fund

The New Mexico Community Foundation

Founded in 2001 with a generous grant from the Oristaglio Foundation, Etruscan Press is a nonprofit cooperative of poets and writers working to produce and promote books that nurture the dialogue among genres, achieve a distinctive voice, and reshape the literary and cultural histories of which we are a part.

etruscan press
www.etruscanpress.org

Etruscan Press books may be ordered from

Consortium Book Sales and Distribution
800.283.3572
www.cbsd.con

Small Press Distribution
800.869.7553
www.spdbooks.com

Etruscan Press is a 501(c)(3) nonprofit organization.
Contributions to Etruscan Press are tax deductible
as allowed under applicable law.
For more information, a prospectus,
or to order one of our titles,
contact us at books@etruscanpress.org.